A Special Educator's Guide to Vocational Training

A Special Educator's Guide to Vocational Training

By

ROBERT A. WEISGERBER, Ed.D.

American Institutes for Research
in the Behavioral Sciences
Palo Alto, California

CHARLES C THOMAS • PUBLISHER

Springfield • Illinois • U.S.A.

Published and Distributed Throughout the World by

CHARLES C THOMAS • PUBLISHER
Bannerstone House
301-327 East Lawrence Avenue, Springfield, Illinois, U.S.A.

ISBN 0-398-03938-0

Library of Congress Catalog Card Number: 79-13684

With THOMAS BOOKS *careful attention is given to all details of manufacturing and design. It is the Publisher's desire to present books that are satisfactory as to their physical qualities and artistic possibilities and appropriate for their particular use.* THOMAS BOOKS *will be true to those laws of quality that assure a good name and good will.*

Printed in the United States of America
V-R-1

Library of Congress Cataloging in Publication Data

Weisgerber, Robert A.
A special educator's guide to vocational training.

Bibliography: p. 199
Includes index.
1. Handicapped children--Vocational education.
I. Title.
LC4019.7.W44 371.9'1 79-13684
ISBN 0-398-03938-0

PREFACE

THIS is a book for special educators who, as a result of new legislation and societal trends, are increasingly being called upon to work with vocational educators in the provision of educational services for handicapped persons. To function effectively in a team relationship, it is useful for special educators to understand the general organizational patterns and instructional processes that characterize vocational education programs. It is important, too, that they recognize the important roles that special educators can play in supporting vocational educators (as well as persons involved in career education, counseling, etc.) as they strive to prepare their students for occupational entry and advancement.

In an earlier volume, *Vocational Education: Teaching the Handicapped Student in Regular Classes,* published by the Council for Exceptional Children, this writer and others attempted to familiarize vocational educators with some of the new perspectives and information they needed to interact effectively with handicapped students and special educators. The present book recognizes the need of special educators to learn more about vocational education so that they can respond intelligently and imaginatively when called upon by vocational educators, who see them as valuable resource persons — educators who know the handicapped person best.

Consideration will be given to the influence that changes in social awareness about the handicapped have had on legislative action; the influence of resulting legislative mandates upon educators' responsibilities; the influence of educators' behaviors on the handicapped persons they serve; and the end result of these influences in terms of job opportunities, job performance, and general living skills of the handicapped.

Throughout, the book will emphasize the need for a "can do" attitude by special educators and vocational educators as they function in a team relationship. At the same time, a pragmatic view will be advanced, which acknowledges that implementation problems will arise but maintains that they need not become insurmountable barriers.

Finally, the writer assumes that the special educators and vocational educators are professionals in their respective fields. No attempt is made to "teach them their own business." Rather, the writer will draw freely from examples of special education and vocational education practice to suggest ways in which the efforts of these professionals can be mutually reinforcing and complementary. Again, this book has been written primarily *for* special educators *about* vocational education; thus it will approach most issues from the special educators' point of view.

Part I, Chapter 1, examines the challenge ahead, points out the philosophic "can do" attitude that underlies the content in the book, and emphasizes the role of teamwork and cooperation that appears to offer the best chance for engendering success in the instructional context and later on the job.

As a baseline for action, it is important to become familiar with the nature of legislation affecting the rights of handicapped persons to receive vocational services. Chapter 2 should provide that familiarization in terms of vocational legislation, exceptional child legislation, rehabilitation legislation, and other legislation that bears directly on the training or education of handicapped persons.

Chapter 3 emphasizes the structure of vocational education and relates this to alternative program opportunities that are likely to be increasingly serving the handicapped. Also discussed in the chapter is the impact of career education and the relationship of occupational clusters to personal and school programming, including pre-vocational and vocational experiences.

Part II, Chapter 4, is concerned with the important role of evaluation in decision making at a number of key points in the special education/vocational education spectrum of service to the individual.

Chapter 5 discusses the Individualized Educational Program (IEP) as a planning tool and the equally important use of vocational assessment for planning purposes. Illustrations are offered of some of the forms, and procedures are described that can facilitate these activities.

Chapter 6 looks at the problems of curriculum design and the implementation of instruction. Various techniques are suggested to develop a framework of individualized study in the context of regular vocational classes. The chapter includes portions on objectives and goal setting, overcoming barriers, and evaluating interim student progress, which has impact on the modification of the instructional strategy and the student's longer range success.

Part III, Chapter 7, reviews the problems and the potentials of the school-to-work transition. Special attention is given to the importance of understanding the employer's point of view and helping to alleviate his or her doubts about the handicapped as productive employees.

Chapter 8 discusses various dimensions of the school-to-work transition, including establishing work readiness and job placement alternatives, and follow-up and support on the job.

Part IV provides additional forms that can be used to facilitate many of the steps and tasks that are implicit in any carefully conceived vocational plan meant to serve handicapped students. Hopefully, these sample materials will be thought provoking and will lead to the adaptation of local forms and procedures in line with the law and with local interests.

In sum, this volume is meant to provide new ideas on which local special education and vocational education staff can build as they jointly design their own delivery systems for the handicapped in vocational education.

ACKNOWLEDGMENTS

IN developing this book, the writer drew heavily upon experiences, information, and personal contacts that were developed in a research study, carried out with support from the Bureau of Occupational and Adult Education, United States Office of Education, which resulted in instructional modules for use by vocational education staff as they begin to work with handicapped students in their regular vocational classes. During the course of that earlier study I was fortunate to make the acquaintance of vocational educators and special educators who helped me "tune in" on the need for interdisciplinary teamwork and gave me many ideas about how this could be accomplished efficiently and effectively. Without attempting to name them all I would like to express my thanks for their valuable insights and suggestions.

Similarly, and of fundamental importance, I would like to acknowledge the influence that my associations with handicapped persons have had on my thinking. In the course of repeatedly observing their adaptability, resourcefulness, persistence, and talents I have come to realize that we who are nonhandicapped have rarely learned to maximize our own capabilities to reach our full potential. I thank my disabled friends, acquaintances, and the students I have observed for their inspiration and their example.

I would be remiss if I failed to acknowledge the role that the American Institutes for Research in the Behavioral Sciences has played in the development of this book. In encouraging me over the years to seek research funding for a wide variety of projects, Doctor Albert B. Chalupsky has helped me to develop a perspective on the challenges facing the handicapped, a perspective that cuts across handicapping conditions and bridges individual, local, state, and federal levels of concern. The work of Doctor John C. Flanagan in furthering the individualization of education has been an influence on my professional priorities and has served as a reminder that I should maintain a mutual interest in the technological and the behavioral dimensions of instructional problems. I am particularly appreciative of the constructive interactions I have had with Doctor Peter Dahl, who has been doing a considerable amount of project work in the same general topical area. Also playing a key role was Doctor William V. Clemans, who encouraged the writing of this book and helped me to arrange for some time off from my regular duties.

Lastly, since this book was written at home rather than at work, I would like to acknowledge the role of my family. My wife, Adrienne, not only put up with my preoccupation and clutter, but she managed to find time in her own busy schedule to type most of the manuscript. Our children, Laraine and Scott, did without some of their Dad's attention and allowed me to "hole up" in the study, thus contributing to my concentration. Since this is the fourth book that we have "shared" as a family, I know how much their quiet support can mean.

R.A.W.

CONTENTS

PART IV
SUPPLEMENTAL FORMS

A Special Educator's Guide to Vocational Training

PART I

THE RATIONALE, MANDATE, AND STRUCTURE OF VOCATIONAL EDUCATION FOR THE HANDICAPPED

CHAPTER 1

THE CHALLENGE AHEAD

AS will be made clear in subsequent chapters of this book, the handicapped citizen is a full citizen, with the full entitlements that such citizenship implies. The access of the handicapped citizen to appropriate publicly supported educational services is well established both in the law and in the courts.

Two landmark judicial decisions in 1972 made very clear that this entitlement is undiminished either by the type of handicapping condition or by its severity. In a class action suit involving the *Pennsylvania Association for Retarded Children v. Commonwealth of Pennsylvania,* District Judge Masterson presiding, it was concluded that

> all mentally retarded persons are capable of benefitting from a program of education and training; that the greatest number of retarded persons given such education and training, are capable of achieving self-sufficiency and the remaining few, with such education and training are capable of achieving some degree of self-care; that the earlier such education and training begins, the more thoroughly and the more efficiently a mentally retarded person benefits from it and, whether begun early or not, that a mentally retarded person can benefit at any point in his life and development from a program of education. (Barbacovi and Clelland, 1977)

In a civil suit involving *Mills v. Board of Education of the District of Columbia,* Judge Waddy supported the plaintiff's claim to equal protection under the law. He concluded that the Supreme Court had previously (*Hobson v. Hansen,* 1967) linked the due process clause of the fourteenth amendment with the fifth amendment, stating that ". . . the court draws the conclusion that the doctrine of equal educational opportunity — the equal protection clause in its application to public school education — is in its full sweep a component of due process binding on the District . . ."

These and other decisions, together with increasing parental pressure and professional support, have done much to shape the nature and content of more recent federal legislation.

The Education for All Handicapped Children Act, Public Law 94-142, is a pervasive, culminating piece of legislation, reflecting as it does the philosophical position of special educators and others concerned with the social, emotional, intellectual, and economic well-being of handicapped persons. Public Law 94-142 states in unequivocal terms the kinds of systematic procedures that should be occurring for *all* students if they are to receive quality education in accordance with their individual differences, needs, and interests. This law will be discussed more fully in the next chapter, but it is important to note that it has the effect of preventing the sole delegation of education for the handicapped to special educators and clearly states that it is the *joint* responsibility of general and special education to meet the educational needs of these persons. In other words, it is no longer legally possible for a regular educator, including a vocational educator, to deny a handicapped person access to a class composed of nonhandicapped students if there is evidence to suggest that the handicapped person could benefit from participation. Moreover, P.L. 94-142 indicates that decisions about the benefits of this participation are to be arrived at through systematic evaluative procedures. Decisions as to the feasibility of participation are the responsibility of a professional placement team, which is to include the parent and, whenever appropriate, the child. Consensus rather than personal opinion, then, will play an increasingly large part in the determination of whether a particular handicapped child will benefit from participation in regular (albeit modified) vocational training or will best be served in a special training program.

Of course, legislation cannot guarantee that "quality" education will take place, or such would have been legislated long ago. Rather, quality education is a consequence of competence, teamwork, and positive attitudes shared by persons who interact with the students. Public Law 94-142 involves such major changes in procedures, particularly for regular educators, that it is understandable that a substantial amount of resistance would be encountered.

OVERCOMING RESISTANCE THROUGH POSITIVE ATTITUDES

An attitude can be defined as a tendency, predisposition, or inclination to respond, act, or behave in an evaluative or judgmental way toward something. That something can be a person, a concept, or even an administrative directive that affects one's customary instructional priorities.

People's attitudes are not always readily apparent, but many times are revealed by their gestures, statements, and other observable behaviors. Identifying attitudes is tricky though, for not all actions an individual makes are attributable to that person's attitude. Similarly, the reason for an action may be quite different than what the observer thinks it is. For example, a teacher who is overly solicitous of someone who is handicapped may appear to the casual observer to have a positive attitude toward that person, but may actually be reflecting a pre-conceived idea about the helplessness of that handicapped person.

In understanding and dealing with attitudes it is important to realize that

- attitudes predict behavior. A teacher who speaks resentfully about having a handicapped person in the class will be inclined to let that resentment be reflected in his or her interactions with that student.
- attitudes tend to generalize themselves. A teacher who has had a favorable (or unfavorable) experience with a handicapped student will more likely expect a similar result with another student, even if the handicap and the student's values and abilities are completely different.
- attitudes can be contagious. The way in which students in a class respond to a handicapped person is apt to be influenced by what they have observed in their teacher's behavior.
- attitudes are formed and changed through experience. A satisfying sense of accomplishment gained through helping a handicapped student develop a useful skill will reinforce a positive attitude toward accepting even greater

instructional challenges.

In each of the principles cited above, it is immediately apparent that if positive attitudes are to be the *outcome*, then the building of positive experiences should be emphasized from the outset. When a handicapped person has been "mainstreamed" in with regular students, a certain amount of difficulties can be expected. Steps should be taken to reduce the occurrence of situations that are destined to lead to failures, bitterness, and the formation of negative attitudes. The reduction of such occurrences does not, of course, mean a policy of avoidance and rejection of the handicapped student, but rather underscores the need for anticipation of difficulties, followed by constructive intervention to encourage a desirable outcome.

Since attitudes are something *people* have, it follows that attitudes of any participant in the "mainstreaming" process can have effects upon others in the group and, therefore, upon the outcome. A thoughtful consideration of presently held attitudes, then, should include attitudes exhibited by (a) both the special education teacher and the vocational education instructor, (b) counselors, administrators, peers and classmates, or others who may be involved in some significant way, (c) the parents, and (d) the handicapped student.

To the extent that attitude improvement seems warranted, it is important to establish the reason(s) that the individual(s) developed their point of view, then plan accordingly. Thus a lack of understanding about the activities and potentials of vocational education for the handicapped student has prevented many special educators from developing a positive attitude about becoming more deeply involved in this part of the curriculum. For the vocational educator the most common reason for a negative attitude is a fear of the unknown, particularly a lack of knowledge about the handicapping condition and about appropriate instructional techniques that he or she could use. Counselors, principals, and significant others may be overly concerned about the risks involved, either anticipating an adverse reaction from teachers or students, or thinking that there is a heightened chance for an accident to take place. Peers may focus on the appearance aspects of the handicap, perhaps finding it repugnant and somehow frightening, while ignoring the deeper positive qualities of the handicapped individual that often enable him or her to overcome or compensate for that adversity. Finally, the handicapped person is susceptible to negative attitudes arising from previous rejections and unfair treatment. Sometimes this feeling is expressed in a pattern of hostility and/or withdrawal, but rarely to an extent that cannot be overcome with patience, understanding, and the provision of ample opportunities for successful accomplishment.

Realistically, then, negative attitudes frequently arise either from assumptions about the "problems" surrounding education of handicapped persons, from resistance to administratively directed changes in procedures and priorities, or simply from interpersonal experiences and viewpoints. Dwelling on the negative side of things is likely to be much less productive, however, than building upon strengths and successes. For example, while gathering information about vocational training of the handicapped in some fourteen California school districts and services organizations for use in a series of teacher training modules, it was readily apparent to this writer that in nearly every instance the success of this integration had far exceeded expectations of the participants. Further, the majority of the vocational educators had (1) volunteered for further assignments of handicapped persons to their classes, (2) actively proselytized other teachers, encouraging them to become involved, and (3) maintained their interest in the progress of the students after they had completed the classes.

In later sections of this book, further attention will be given to shaping positive attitudes. Numerous examples will be given to make clear the importance of optimism and a "can do" philosophy.

COOPERATION AND TEAMWORK

Implicit in the approach being recommended in this book is the fundamental idea of coordination among those persons charged with providing meaningful educational opportunities for handicapped students, and cooperation between educators and employers in providing meaningful work experiences for these students. Recapping the comments in the preceding section, this requires the breaking down of resistance rooted in tradition and habit, reduction of ignorance, and the elimination of "domain" guarding.

Teamwork implies a sharing of the responsibilities for counseling, instructional design, monitoring student growth, and assessment of the development of job-relevant skills. Throughout the steps of planning, instruction, and placement in work situations, it is essential that the service delivery team apply its energies efficiently and within a framework that recognizes the *unique individuality of each handicapped student.* A number of guidelines will be suggested throughout the book that encourage instructional flexibility in accordance with individual differences while meeting the requirements for equity and fairness as directed in the new legislation.

Ultimately, then, this book is concerned with individual students, whose future lives as productive, contributing adults are in a very real way shaped by the willingness of vocational educators and special educators to work together, and enhanced by their knowledge of their respective, complementary roles.

CHAPTER 2

ACCESS TO VOCATIONAL TRAINING BY THE HANDICAPPED

TRENDS AND LEGISLATIVE MANDATES

The Changing Scope of Vocational Education

NOT too many years ago there was a reluctance on the part of many educators and many students to become involved in vocational education. The shop teacher and the student in shop class often found themselves relegated to a second-class status within the school environment, and the vocational curriculum reflected this modest stature. In the last decade the vocational education movement has come a long, long way; now many vocational facilities have waiting lists of applicants. By learning to take advantage of their ties with business and industry, and by attracting increasing amounts of federal support, vocational programs now rank among the strongest and most valuable components of American education.

Illustrative of the way in which vocational programs have matured in the last decade is their organizational representation at the state level, where separate staffs within the state departments of education are charged with developing and implementing multiyear state plans, plans that aim at the articulation of course offerings among and between secondary and college programs. There has been a substantial change in the content of vocational courses over this period, with a shift away from activities such as the making of wooden shoe boxes, metal candle holders, or other marginal items. The shift is toward courses in which skills are learned that have direct application in the world of work, such as lens grinding or floristry. Much of the credit for this change to occupationally oriented training can be traced to two practices, the increased use of advisory councils drawn from business and industry, and the increased awareness of the techniques of task analysis as a means for identifying those skills essential for job success.

These two practices (advisory councils and task analysis) are roughly paralleled in special education by the increasing use of interdisciplinary teams, including parents, and by the trend toward diagnostic-prescriptive approaches for working with handicapped children. Thus, in these and in a number of other ways, the special educator and the vocational educator already have much in common. By building on these commonalities they should be able to relate to each other's priorities and concerns and simultaneously benefit the handicapped persons they both must serve.

Current Vocational Mandates

There is little doubt that the single, most pervasive change in the nature of vocational education is that which is now taking place as a result of the passage of Public Law 94-482. Among the many provisions of this comprehensive Act are a number that will further increase the amount of attention that is given to accountability and to the needs of all students. Major emphasis has been given to the rights of access to vocational education by the handicapped, women, and disadvantaged; in other words, by those who previously were underserved by vocational education. The following excerpts from P.L. 94-482 provide the framework within which vocational educators are to offer equitable services for students, irrespective of their being handicapped or nonhandicapped.

Subsequent portions of this chapter will describe the pertinent aspects of Public Law 94-142, the Education for All Handicapped Children Act, and Public Law 93-112, the Vocational Rehabilitation Act of 1973, as well as the Architectural Barriers Act of 1968. All are linked to each other and affect vocational education of the handicapped.

PUBLIC LAW 94-482

Title II Education Amendments of 1976

As part of an omnibus Act in which a number of educational

programs were amended, the Vocational Education Act of 1963 was extended and expanded. Title II of P.L. 94-482 is divided into Part A — State Vocational Education Programs, Part B — National Programs, and Part C — Definitions. Since the legislation spans some forty-seven pages, it is only possible here to point out certain aspects that concern provision of services to the handicapped, or imply them through inclusive phrasing. Brief comments will be offered with each excerpt, followed by an interpretive summary.

Section 101 makes clear the broad *scope of eligibility* for persons to receive vocational education services, including

> . . . persons of all ages in all communities of the state, those in high school, those that have completed or discontinued their formal education and are preparing to enter the labor market, but need to upgrade their skills or learn new ones, those with special educational handicaps, and those in post-secondary schools. . . .

The passage continues, pointing out the *characteristics of vocational education* to which these persons are guaranteed access:

> . . . will have ready access to vocational training or retraining which is of high quality, which is realistic in the light of actual or anticipated opportunities for gainful employment, and which is suited to their needs, interests, and ability to benefit from such training.

Substantial *funding* is included in Section 102, with authorizations extending through 1982. Yearly total authorizations amount to

$1,160,000,000 for 1979
$1,325,000,000 for 1980
$ 156,325,000 for 1981
$ 156,485,000 for 1982

Specific *state allotments* of funds are assigned in Section 103 to varying age groups (15-19, 20-24, 25-65), to vocational services for Indians, and to support a National Occupational Information Coordinating Committee. Specific sums are earmarked for assisting the states in developing five-year plans, including accountability reports and evaluation studies, and for administering state programs.

Section 105 stipulates that each state is to have an *advisory council* (a majority of which are not educators or administrators) that includes one or more individuals who

> . . . have special knowledge, experience, or qualifications with respect to the special educational needs of physically or mentally handicapped persons. . . .

Further, each eligible recipient of funds to operate vocational education programs must establish local advisory councils, with special emphasis on including representatives of business, industry, and labor. (It is not uncommon that these local advisory councils also include someone who is highly knowledgeable about employment of the handicapped. Often this is a person who employs them already or is actively participating in a multibusiness placement program in cooperation with schools.)

In *distributing funds to local educational agencies,* Section 106 specifies that the states will use as the two most important factors in determining this distribution

> (I) . . . the relative financial ability of (local education) agencies to provide the resources necessary . . . and the relative number of low-income families or individuals within such agencies, and
> (II) . . . the relative number or concentration of students whom they serve whose education imposes higher than average costs, such as handicapped students . . . .

This approach makes clear that extra burdens are not placed on local districts as a result of services to the handicapped, because the extent of this special needs constituency is to be taken into account as a criterion before funds are distributed.

Section 107 concerns the *five year state plan* and states that it shall

> . . . set out explicitly the uses which the State intends to make of these funds to meet the special needs of handicapped and disadvantaged persons and persons who have limited English speaking ability . . . .

Under the heading "National Priority Programs," Section 110 specifies *funding for the handicapped:*

> . . . For each fiscal year, at least 10 per centum of each state's

> allotment under section 103 shall be used to pay 50 per centum of the cost of vocational education for handicapped persons.

In other words, a minimum level of financial assistance for vocational education of the handicapped within a state would mean that half of the costs would be borne by vocational education funds, and that the total of these vocational funds made available within the state can be no less than 10 percent of the total amount of money made available to the state for vocational education purposes . . . a very substantial sum.

Of special significance to educators of the handicapped, who themselves are keenly aware of the Education for All Handicapped Children Act, P.L. 94-142, is the provision that funds for handicapped students must be *expended in accordance with the terms of P.L. 94-142.* Section 106, mentioned previously, states

> . . . that the funds used for purposes of section 110 (a) are consistent with the State plan pursuant to section 613 (a) of the Education for the Handicapped Act.

This Act will be summarized in the next section of this chapter.

A number of types of grants are authorized in P.L. 94-482 under the heading of Program Improvement and Support Services (20% of each state's allotment). Section 132, which deals with *exemplary and innovative programs,* an important aspect of program improvement and support services (subpart 3 of the Act), again reminds us of the priority that is given to the needs of the handicapped. Specifically, it calls for

> . . . programs designed to broaden occupational aspirations and opportunities for youth, with special emphasis given to youth who have academic, socioeconomic, or other handicaps . . . .

Moreover, Section 132 makes elementary as well as secondary students eligible for such services.

Also, under the program improvement and support services subpart, but dealing with *curriculum development,* Section 133 suggests the appropriateness of expenditures for

> . . . development and dissemination of vocational education

> curriculum materials for new and changing occupational fields and for individuals with special needs . . . .

This clearly encourages the development and sharing of materials and techniques designed to be effective for the handicapped.

Section 134 continues this program improvement focus and recognizes the need for appropriate *vocational guidance and counseling,* including

> . . . establishment of vocational resource centers to meet the special need of out-of-school individuals, including individuals seeking second careers, individuals entering the job market late in life, handicapped individuals, individuals from economically depressed communities or areas, or early retirees . . . .

Section 150, which relates to *consumer and homemaking education* (Subpart 5) specifically encourages

> . . . outreach programs in communities for youth and adults giving considerations to special needs such as, but not limited to, aged, young children, school-age parents, single parents, handicapped persons, educationally disadvantaged persons and programs connected with health care delivery systems . . . .

Up to this point our review of the Act has centered on the ramifications of various sections on state and local vocational programs. It is interesting and significant to note that Part B of the Act, which deals with national programs, continues in much the same manner. Thus the National Advisory Council must also include among its members a person who is experienced in education and training of the handicapped. There are a number of national priorities and concerns within the discretion of the Commissioner, such as research and evaluation studies that take cognizance of the special needs of the handicapped. Also included are provisions for training and advanced study in vocational education, with stipends of up to $4,500 per academic year and $1,000 per summer session. It is interesting to note that, following comments from the field, the portion of the Regulations* pertaining to Vocational Education Personnel Training was amended to specifically include (among the categories of training that are allowable) the

---

*Federal Register, October 3, 1977.

training of vocational educators in the teaching of the handicapped and disadvantaged.

Finally, in Part 3 of the Act, which deals with definitions, the term *handicapped* is defined, for eligibility purposes, as follows:

> . . . the term "handicapped," when applied to persons, means persons who are mentally retarded, hard of hearing, deaf, speech impaired, visually impaired, seriously emotionally disturbed, crippled, or other health impaired persons who by reason thereof require special education and related services, and who, because of their handicapping condition, cannot succeed in the regular vocational education program without special education assistance or who require a modified vocational education program.

Summary of P.L. 94-482

It should be clear to the reader that the many references to the handicapped throughout Title II, Vocational Education, preclude any deliberate or *de facto* failure, either by the states or by local school programs, to provide appropriate vocational services. The key ideas and provisions are as follows:

- Persons with handicaps are eligible, regardless of their age, what community they live in, whether they have completed high school, whether they are employed or unemployed, or whether they want to learn new skills or upgrade old ones.
- They are entitled to quality vocational training or retraining that is suited to their needs, interests, and abilities.
- Planning and advisory groups are to include representation by persons familiar with the educational needs of the handicapped.
- Proportionately more funds are to be allocated by the state to those programs having a higher concentration of special needs persons in their enrollment.
- At least one dollar of every ten in the state allotment for vocational education is to be used for the needs of handicapped persons, and the uses the state will make of these funds are to be spelled out in a five-year plan.

- Expenditures are to be in accordance with the provisions of P.L. 94-142, the Education for All Handicapped Children Act.
- The areas of program improvement in which special needs/handicapped persons are named as deserving priority attention include (a) exemplary and innovative programs, (b) curriculum development, and (c) vocational guidance and counseling.
- Outreach programs for handicapped persons in the community are encouraged for the purpose of consumer and homemaking education.
- The remodeling and renovation of facilities to accommodate the handicapped are now required.

PUBLIC LAW 94-142

The Education for all Handicapped Children Act of 1975

Public Law 94-142 is a landmark piece of legislation as far as the handicapped are concerned. It is comprehensive, strongly worded, and clearly aimed at the guaranteeing of full access to appropriate educational services, at public expense, by handicapped persons ages 3 through 18 by September 1, 1978 and 3 through 21 by September 1, 1980. Specifically the law requires states to establish

> . . . procedures to assure that, to the maximum extent appropriate, handicapped children, including children in public and private institutions or other care facilities, are educated with children who are not handicapped, and that special classes, separate schooling or other removal of handicapped children from the regular education environment occurs only when the nature or severity of the handicap is such that education in regular classes with the use of supplementary aids and services cannot be achieved satisfactorily . . . . [Section 612, (5)(B)]

There is a clear tie between P.L. 94-142 and the vocational education legislation under which state and local vocational programs operate. Section 613 of P.L. 94-142 requires that each state plan developed pursuant to the Act shall

> . . . provide that programs and procedures will be established to assure that funds received by the State or any of its political subdivisions under any Federal program, including . . . the Vocational Education Act of 1963 (20 USC 1262 (a) (4) (B), under which there is specific authority for the provision of assistance for the education of handicapped children, will be utilized by the State, or any of its political subdivisions, only in a manner consistent with the goal of providing a free appropriate public education for all handicapped children . . . . [Section 613, (a)(2)]

It is important to realize that the legislation does *not* say that every handicapped student must receive vocational education but rather that access to regular vocational education is (a) as much the right of a handicapped student as a nonhandicapped one, (b) predicated on what is best for the child, in no way giving an option of acceptance or rejection to the designated teacher, and (c) consistent with the goal of providing a free, appropriate education for the handicapped.

Within these three key ideas is nested a series of assumptions that are also spelled out in the Act, including

- the requirement of alternative placement possibilities including instruction in regular classes, special classes, special schools, home instruction, and instruction in hospitals and institutions, with the emphasis being given to placement in the *least restrictive environment* from which the child could benefit;
- the requirement for *due process,* including parental rights of access to information, written notice, participation in meetings concerning the child's placement, presence of counsel, fairness in rulings, independent evaluation, presentation of evidence, processes of appeal and civil court adjudication with award of damages in adverse rulings;
- the requirement for an *individualized educational program* (IEP), which is in written form and includes a statement of the child's present level of performance, a list of annual goals and short-term objectives, a specification of the edu-

cational services, media, and materials to be provided, a statement of the extent to which the child will participate in regular educational classes, including the duration of the services, and the objective criteria and evaluation procedures for determining at least annually whether the objectives were achieved.

It is especially noteworthy that the developing, reviewing, and revising of individual education programs are to be carried out at the local level through meetings involving

- an LEA representative (other than the child's teachers) who is qualified in special education services;
- teachers (special, regular, or both) having a direct responsibility for implementing the individualized educational program for that child;
- one or both of the child's parents, or a parent surrogate;
- other individuals at the discretion of the LEA or the parent;
- when appropriate, the child.

While no mention is made of the vocational educator participating in these meetings, this possibility is implicit since the regular teacher category clearly includes vocational educators. If the responsibility for the provision of vocational services to a particular child is assigned to a regular vocational teacher, it is quite reasonable (and logical) to assume that that teacher should be requested to participate in developing, reviewing, and revising of the child's individual educational program.

Public Law 94-142 takes cognizance of the importance of having well-informed, qualified instructional personnel delivering the specified educational services to the handicapped child. In this regard, the state plan must describe programs and procedures for

> . . . (A) the development and implementation of a comprehensive system of personnel development which shall include the inservice training of general and special educational instructional and support personnel, detailed procedures to assure that all personnel necessary to carry out the purposes of this Act are appropriately and adequately prepared and trained,

> and effective procedures for acquiring and disseminating to teachers and administrators of programs for handicapped children significant information derived from educational research, demonstration, and similar projects, and (B) adopting, where appropriate, promising educational practices and materials development through such projects . . . . [Section 613 (a) (3)]

Additionally, the Act vests within the Commissioner's office the power to award grants for the removal of architectural barriers upon application of any state or local educational agency or intermediate education unit. These funds are to be used for alteration of buildings and equipment in a manner consistent with P.L. 90-480, relating to architectural barriers. The Act goes on to provide special authorizations for centers on educational media and materials for the handicapped. Finally, it requires recipients of assistance under the Act to make positive efforts to employ and advance handicapped persons.

Substantial funds are provided within the law for use by states with approved plans. The federal government is scheduled to contribute an increasing percentage of the excess costs of providing this special education — 10 percent in the school year 1978-1979, 20 percent in 1979-1980, 30 percent in 1980-1981, and 40 percent in 1981-1982 and thereafter. Local education agencies are assured of receiving 75 percent of the money sent to each state, on a pass-through basis. In terms of amounts, the legislation provides (in year 1978-1979) for some $535 million, or about $140 extra per child served.

Summary of P.L. 94-142

Although vocational educators may not have heard about or know the details of the Education for All Handicapped Children Act, they are certain to be affected by it. Regardless of whether they have had prior experience or personal feelings about teaching handicapped students along with their regular students, this law directs that they will be called upon to do so in compliance with the "least restrictive environment" concept. The law further stipulates that services be appropriate and in the form of written "Individual Educational Programs." This very clearly means both a tailoring of the instructional approach and the use of appropriate assessment procedures to reveal progress toward pre-stated short-term and long-term objectives for each handicapped individual.

Much attention must be given to the joint planning of any specific vocational education experiences that are to be provided to any particular student, and there is a mandated involvement of parents in any deliberations substantially affecting the child's program planning and implementation.

REHABILITATION ACT OF 1973, P.L. 93-112

Federal and State Supported Rehabilitation

The responsibility of government, both at the federal and state level, in providing vocational training and placement for handicapped persons is a well-acknowledged fact. For a number of years Departments of Rehabilitation in the various states have concentrated on enhancing the vocational viability of handicapped persons and on the development of a cadre of trained vocational counselors to carry out this work. These federally mandated programs have undergone a number of changes in recent years, including a change in the name itself with the dropping of "Vocational" from the departmental title. This should not be taken as an indication that vocational priorities no longer exist, but rather that other aspects of daily living, personal independence, and self-reliance are acknowledged as well.

Another change that has taken place over the years is the broadening of the clientele to be served. This broadening has been in terms of (a) services for school-aged handicapped persons in addition to those who are already adults (b) inclusion of alcoholics and drug addicts along with the physically impaired and mentally impaired, and (c) inclusion of the severely handicapped, whose problems of vocational preparation and gainful employment are not readily overcome. Each of these changes has taken place in spite of controversy and difficulty surrounding their implementation. For example, the support of school-aged student's needs raises jurisdictional questions with respect to the role of the schools. What has evolved, however, and generally quite successfully, is a close working relationship between the two types of agencies, with the local office of the Rehabilitation Department responding cooperatively to schools' requests, particularly in the areas of special testing, short-term training (such as orientation and mobility help), transportation, and prosthetic appliances when such services are related to the development of an individual's vocational potential.

In the second type of change, it should be noted that *not* every defect or "handicap" is qualifying, but rather that the individual (1) has an impairment that will substantially limit employment and (2) can reasonably benefit from vocational rehabilitation services. That is, impairments that limit one or more major life activities, such as caring for oneself, performing manual tasks, walking, seeing, hearing, breathing, learning, or working, but which do not preclude the latter. Thus the rehabilitation process is consciously focused on those individuals who would have little chance of functioning independently or of entering into gainful employment in the absence of subsidized, professional help.

The third change has come about in part because of client dissatisfaction with the idea that the prospect of gainful employment had to be apparent, and the handicap clearly surmountable, before services would be made available. This placement-potential criterion had led, in the past, to the acceptance of "easy" cases and denial of "difficult" cases. It obviously was discriminatory against those persons who most needed help.

Perhaps nowhere has the change in philosophy been more apparent than in California, where Ed Roberts, a quadraplegic who earlier had been turned away by the old California Department of Vocational Rehabilitation as being unemployable, has now become head of the revamped state-wide Rehabilitation Department. Understandably, he pursues a strong affirmative policy of priority services for the severely handicapped. As indicated previously, a broader view of life-needs has been taken, with the result that the priority now includes the development of independent living skills. Certainly, a balanced approach is necessary whenever it can be shown that the person needs to develop new skills and/or receive special equipment before being able to adequately care for himself or herself *off* the job as well as *on* it.

Coordination of Services

Among the many provisions in the Act, two are of special significance to special and vocational educators inasmuch as they are in keeping with the requirements for individualization of educational programs as stated in P.L. 94-142, and the emphasis on work study and cooperative education programs as spelled out in P.L. 94-482. Referred to are Section 101 (B) (9), which calls for the writing of an individualized written rehabilitation program for each client, a process that is compatible, though nonoverlapping, with the IEP required in the schools; and Section 101 (B) (11), which calls for cooperative efforts with other agencies, including local public agencies, that are providing services to the handicapped and are employment related.

Envision, then, a blind student in his or her senior year in high school, whose IEP includes a component of vocational training and work experience preparatory to that person's seeking gainful employment upon graduation. Suppose too that the occupational area in which the handicapped person was interested, and was generally qualified to enter, involved the frequent need to read ink print, along with other skills in which reading was not essential. Assume also that the individual's family is in economic need and that the school's resources are such that the purchase of an electronic device costing several thousand dollars in not possible, even though that device could, with appropriate special training, enable the individual to read ink print directly rather than depend on its conversion into braille. Perhaps the vocational work experience coordinator has even located an employer who is willing to give the student part-time employment restricted to those parts of the job not requiring use of ink print materials (in effect agreeing to a temporary job redesign). However, the employer indicates to the work experience coordinator and to the student that full employment would not be possible since the "whole job" requires ink print reading skills. In circumstances such as these it would be quite appropriate to have the student establish his or her eligibility for rehabilitation services and then cooperatively arrange (with the vocational rehabilitation counselor) for the student's acquisition of a device for ink print reading, together with training in its use, under the terms of P.L. 93-112.

Scope of Services

Instances such as the preceding example of cooperative effort are becoming more numerous as special and vocational educators realize the many ways that the Rehabilitation Department can help them serve the handicapped student. As spelled out in Section 103 of the Act, the goods and services available to the handicapped include, but are not limited to, the following:

1. Diagnostic and related services for evaluating rehabilitation potential;
2. Counseling, guidance, referral, placement, follow-up and follow-along services after employment;
3. Vocational and training services and materials (except that higher education services would be provided only after attempting to obtain grant assistance from other sources);
4. Physical and mental restorative services, including surgery, hospitalization, prosthetic and orthotic devices, special services such as dialysis, and diagnosis and treatment by physicians and licensed psychologists;
5. Subsistence maintenance during rehabilitation;
6. Interpreter services and reader services;
7. Recruitment and training services to acquaint the handicapped with new employment opportunities;
8. Orientation and mobility training for the blind;
9. Occupational licenses, tools, equipment, and initial stocks of supply;
10. Transportation in connection with the provision of rehabilitation services;
11. Telecommunications, sensory, and other technological aids.

This spirit of cooperation has proved quite effective in such schools as Selaco-Downey High School in Los Angeles County, widely known for its services both to deaf and hard-of-hearing students as well as to a large, regular student body. Selaco-Downey has been able to sustain its high-quality program partly due to its ongoing working relationship with the Rehabilitation Department, including designation of particular vocational rehabilitation counselors with whom the school staff could work in a team manner.

Rehabilitation in a New Light — Title V

The Rehabilitation Act of 1973 was much more than a renewal of the concept of rehabilitation services and a streamlining and expansion of the scope of services to be provided. For good reason, Title V of the Act has been referred to as the "Bill of Rights for disabled people." Containing Sections 501 through 504, all of which are significant, it can be stated that Section 504 has become the most compelling and significant part of the entire Act. The following discussion describes the purpose of each of the Sections and then deals in extended detail with Section 504.

Section 501: Establishes an Interagency Committee on Handicapped Employees at the Federal level, and requires agencies to institute affirmative action programs for hiring the handicapped.

Section 502: Establishes an Architectural and Transportation Barriers Compliance Board to investigate barriers and recommend actions and alternative approaches to the President and the Congress.

Section 503: Requires Federal and prime contractual agreements (of over $2500) to contain a provision for affirmative action in the hiring and advancement of qualified handicapped persons.

Section 504: Provides for nondiscrimination in any program or activity, as stated below.

> No otherwise qualified handicapped individual in the United States, as defined in section 7 (6), shall solely by

reason of his handicap, be excluded from the participation in, be denied the benefits of, or be subjected to discrimination under any program or activity receiving Federal financial assistance.

While each of the sections contained in the Act is important, there can be little doubt that Section 504 is the cornerstone of a number of environmental and social changes currently taking place and continuing at least through 1980, by which time even structural changes to existing buildings must be completed.

Even though it had long been in the legislation and clearly was designed to protect the handicapped from the abuses arising out of ignorance, prejudice, and superficial judgments, Section 504 remained dormant until April 28, 1977, when regulations for implementing it were signed by the Secretary of Health, Education, and Welfare, Joseph Califano. Ironically, and perhaps with some measure of poetic justice, the handicapped themselves were responsible for the final issuance of the regulations by "lobbying" in a most persuasive way, actually camping out in federal buildings until there was agreement that the government would "put teeth" into the various provisions of the Act by enforcement of Section 504.

Implementation of the Mandate Against Discrimination

Following the issuance of the HEW regulations, which had the effect of departmentwide impact, an Executive order (11914) by President Nixon extended the authority of the Secretary to develop a general standard that would be applied to *all* government agencies. As a direct result, other agencies (such as those concerned with housing and transportation) have been actively developing their own Section 504 regulations.

Summary of P.L. 93-112 — Selected Implications for Education

- All handicapped persons are entitled to benefit from free pre-school, elementary, secondary, and adult educational services, including those outside the 3-21 year age range as covered by P.L. 94-142. Postsecondary and vocational education services are specifically directed to serve any handicapped person who meets the academic and technical standards requisite to admission. (Technical standards refers to all nonacademic admissions criteria, fairly applied.)

- Admission tests cannot be used if they have an adverse effect on handicapped persons unless the test can be shown to predict success and no alternative test is available. Test time must be extended if necessitated by the handicapped person's inability to respond at the customary rate. In lieu of such admission testing, educational success may be judged on the basis of first-year performance and supported by periodic validity studies.

Additionally, there can be no quotas of handicapped persons or discriminatory recruiting for vocational education programs. Pre-enrollment questioning about whether the person is handicapped is not allowed unless it is done with the intent of rectifying past injustices and intentionally increasing participation by the handicapped. Even then, it must be made clear in advance that response is voluntary.

- Adjustments must be made in the educational programs as appropriate to the individual. This holds true for curricular and extracurricular programs, and may involve the provision of auxiliary aides, taped texts, special purpose equipment, and special help from nonacademic services such as counseling and placement services. Counseling help cannot be discriminatory, such as the arbitrary restriction of career objectives or stereotypic recommendations about vocational alternatives.
- Housing must be accessible and of the same cost and quality as is available to the other students. No handicapped person can be excluded from participation in program activities that are available to other students solely on the basis of access to the facilities in which the activity is taking place. That is, the facility as a whole must be available, rather than every possible access point being modified. When integration of the handicapped person with the nonhandicapped is not believed to be beneficial, then alternative facilities and programing of equivalent quality are to be made available without cost to the individual, and as close to home as possible.

- Due process procedures are required, with parents' rights of information about identification, evaluation, and placement being fully safeguarded, and rights of appeal must be assured.

In considering the overall implications of the Rehabilitation Act of 1973 and its Section 504, it is evident that there will be participation of the handicapped in the mainstream. Bob Considine picturesquely summarized the trend in his syndicated newspaper column:

> America's newest-grouped minority, the more than 11,000,000 citizens who are physically or mentally handicapped, is on the move, militantly determined never to be ignored again. In wheelchairs, on crutches, and by tapping canes they are advancing toward a day when their rights to better education and equal job opportunities can no longer be denied them . . . . These Americans don't want a hand-out, they demand a hand-up.

ADDITIONAL LEGISLATION RELATED TO THE HANDICAPPED

While the principal legislation affecting the vocational training of the handicapped, their successful transition to gainful employment, and their long-term, self-sustaining independence have been previously discussed at some length, i.e. P.L. 94-142, P.L. 94-482, and P.L. 93-112, there are several other legislative mandates that deserve mention since they may bear on the practical implementation of particular students' individualized educational programs. For the sake of brevity, they are outlined briefly here.

- The Fair Labor Standards Act, as amended in 1974, includes provisions for employment exemptions to the minimum wage for student-learners, student-workers, handicapped workers in sheltered workshops, and handicapped workers in competitive industry, the latter including trainees under Rehabilitation Department and Veterans Administration auspices. It provides for the issuance of certificates authorizing subminimum wage rates in recognition that lower productivity due to a disabling condition would unfairly penalize employers who were willing to employ the handicapped person in spite of their inability to fully perform the job at a rate and/or quality level consistent with other, nonhandicapped new employees. In 1976, for example, some 11,795 certificates were in effect for handicapped workers in competitive industry. In comparison, some 145,442 handicapped workers were employed in certificated sheltered workshops.

It should be kept in mind that the earning of any pay by handicapped persons, including handicapped students, is an important step in their building self-esteem and independence. Eventually, some of these students might be able to develop sufficient skills and efficiency levels to enable them to receive full pay without economic detriment to the employer and in full equity in comparison to other employees' wages. Other handicapped students (for example, students who were unable to be mainstreamed into regular vocational classes) may not reach this goal and will continue to work in sheltered workshops or work activity centers.

Inquiries about this law, procedures for issuance of exemption certificates, and information about specific applicability to local situations in the private sector should be directed to the United States Department of Labor or to the state Employment Development Department.

- ESEA Title I (P.L. 93-380) provides formula grants to Local Education Agencies serving areas with concentrations of low-income families to help meet the needs of educationally deprived students. Prior to this distribution of funds, however, there is a "set aside" of 10 percent of the funds for handicapped children in state-supported and state-operated institutions. In 1978 some 144 state mental health, education, and public welfare agencies received 121.5 million dollars ($553 per child) for such educational services to the handicapped.
- ESEA Title IV-C of the same act is concerned with educational innovation and support. These funds are intended to stimulate state leadership and provide demonstrations of needed educational services. After 15 percent of the funds are used for the state leadership purposes, another 15 percent is earmarked for special programs and projects for

handicapped students. The 1978 funds for handicapped children amount to some twenty-one million dollars.

- The Head Start, Economic Opportunity, and Community Partnership Act (P.L. 93-644) directly supports private and public organizations providing Head Start instructional programs. By law, such programs must make available these instructional services to handicapped children (there is a 10 percent quota to be met). Thus, this is a clear-cut example of the intent to integrate the handicapped into the regular instructional program to the maximum extent possible. In 1977, 36,000 handicapped children were served at a cost of some twenty-nine million dollars.
- Impact Aid, Maintenance, and Operation (P.L. 81-874) is concerned with special payments to schools serving "federally connected" children, including Indian children and children of persons on active duty in the armed services. If the child is handicapped, an allowance that is one and one-half times the regular amount is paid for educational support. In 1978 some 25,000 students received services at a cost of twenty-two million dollars.
- The Indian Education Act (P.L. 93-318) provides funds for competitive grants to agencies, tribes, and organizations for exemplary educational programs, pre-service and in-service training, pilot and demonstration programs, and information dissemination. In 1978 some $8,000,000 was expended for the handicapped under Title IVB of the Act.
- The Education of the Handicapped Act (P.L. 95-49) follows the trend set by the passage of P.L. 94-142, the landmark Education for All Handicapped Children Act, the previous year. In it, funds are allocated for a variety of educational services for the handicapped including regional centers for the deaf-blind, programs for the preschool handicapped and the severely handicapped, and regional vocational, adult, and postsecondary programs. Emphasis in the Act is given to diagnosis, referral, and programming services and to expanded professional training.
- The Tax Reduction and Simplification Act of 1977 (P.L. 95-30) reduces taxes for a significant number of Americans

who use the standard deduction and contains a number of provisions beneficial to handicapped individuals and employers who hire them, including handicapped veterans.

- Recent relevant legislation includes the CETA Amendments of 1978 (P.L. 95-524), the Housing and Community Development Amendments of 1978 (P.L. 95-557), the Elementary and Secondary Education Act (P.L. 95-561), and the Rehabilitation, Comprehensive Services and Developmental Disabilities Amendments of 1978 (HR 12467) signed into law by President Carter on November 6, 1978.

Other Legislation

It is beyond the scope of this chapter to fully list or explore the many pieces of federal legislation that relate, directly or indirectly, to the provision of services for the handicapped. In any case, such a list is ever changing as federal programs are constantly being amended, consolidated, or even closed out. One way to stay abreast of current federal legislation is through the annual listing of the Administration Budget as it is sent to Congress each year. This is published (along with helpful information about other pertinent executive and legislative information) in the *Washington Report*, a newsletter distributed free by the American Foundation for the Blind, Inc., 15 West 16th St., New York, NY, 10011.

CHAPTER 3

STRUCTURING VOCATIONAL EDUCATION TO SERVE THE HANDICAPPED

WHILE the structure of vocational education is neither consistent across states nor across school districts within a given state, there are, nevertheless, some general patterns and emerging trends. One of the more important trends in recent years has been toward an enlightened view of the meaning of work, especially its relationship to the individual's personal fulfillment in a chosen career field. Career development is a broader term than vocational education, embracing as it does such concepts as career awareness and career exploration activities that typically would be expected to precede specific vocational training. While career education concepts are consciously being integrated into course content at the elementary school level, they also extend into adult living where the concepts of career change and career advancement are included. Because of its scope, career education is a plausible place to begin an examination of the structure of vocational education, even though the two terms are far from synonymous.

CAREER EDUCATION AND OCCUPATIONAL CLUSTERS

What is career education? Its definition is not easy, and there is no immediate consensus evident in the definitions offered by acknowledged experts in career education. For example, three definitions drawn from the book *Career Education: What It Is and How to Do It,* by Hoyt, Evans, Mackin, and Mangum (1972), show differences as well as similarities of viewpoint.

Definition #1, attributed to Hoyt, defines career education as

> . . . the total effort of public education and the community aimed at helping all individuals to become familiar with the values of a work-oriented society, to integrate those values into their personal value systems, and to implement these

> values into their lives in such a way that work becomes possible, meaningful, and satisfying to each individual. (P. 1)

Definition #2, attributed to Evans, defines career education as

> . . . the total effort of the community to develop a personally satisfying succession of opportunities for service through work, paid or unpaid, extending throughout life. (P. 1)

Definition #3, which appears as a summary statement in Chapter 6, co-authored by Mangum and Hoyt, defines career education as

> . . . the sum total of those experiences of the individual associated with his choice of, preparation for, entry into, and progress in occupations throughout his occupational life. (P. 182)

It is clear that career education is not a course, but a philosophical stance. It is also clear that it focuses on two processes — developing a work ethic that is satisfying to the individual and making possible a continuum of growth in occupational opportunties for individuals in a work-oriented society. The first of these processes implies the need for early emphasis on helping young students to become cognizant of alternatives in the world of work and helping them to better understand their own interests in relation to those alternatives. The second of these processes implies a need for a high degree of articulation (a) between career education and vocational education programs, (b) across various grade levels of formal schooling, elementary through adult levels, and (c) between the school and the community, including on-the-job training in industry. In other words, what is sought is a system for work-centered lifelong learning of a highly individualistic nature.

Career Education and the Handicapped

There are many similarities in career education for the handicapped and career education for the nonhandicapped. For example, both groups start from a position of naivete concerning the world of work and have not yet organized their thinking relative to various work options. On the other hand, the handicapped, perhaps due to their lack of mobility, or the simple lack of opportunity (as may occur with overprotective or embarrassed parents), will generally be less informed about the kinds of jobs that adults perform than are their nonhandicapped classmates. With a starting point that is obviously "in arrears," it is hardly surprising that the handicapped youngster involved in career education at the elementary level will need more effort on the part of school staff and parents to familiarize him or her with the work concepts. The handicapped youngster will also need more time before he or she will begin to cultivate a curiosity and (eventually) an interest in different occupational areas.

The example of the postman is one of the typical jobs to which nonhandicapped children are exposed rather early, both in real life and in their school studies. There is a good chance that the congenitally blind child will have little concept formation about this person by the time he or she enters first grade, never having seen the postman walking about or driving a mail truck, nor having been sent to the mailbox to fetch the mail. Even the mail itself has little meaning. In school, curriculum materials, such as illustrated books, "community worker" filmstrips, etc., are not of help in developing that child's understanding. There is little doubt, however, that such materials would be of help to develop understanding and awareness on the part of a handicapped child who is deaf or hard of hearing.

To carry this illustration forward, let us assume that a deaf child does develop a curiosity in the postman's job following career education exposure. His or her interests could be explored by involving the child in school activities that are akin to the job duties of the postman, such as delivering school messages or sorting and organizing materials. Job-relevant habits, such as punctuality and dependability, could be developed in a similar manner. In later grades this interest might expand into a tentative choice of a vocational course of study along those lines.

Kokaska (1978) has suggested that the elementary and secondary level years should be organized in four basic areas of career development: (1) career awareness (K-6), (2) career exploration (7-8), (3) career orientation (9-10), and (4) career preparation (11-12). Koskaska is realistic in that he points out the futility of attempting to expose the elementary level child to the "over 20,000 types of occupational categories that exist in the world of work." This would be patently foolish to attempt, and a waste of time for all concerned. What is needed, then, to make Kokaska's K through 12 progression of career education practical, is a strategy in which the student learns about his or her options. In the lower grades, the presumption is that the knowledge about work options expands gradually, and in upper grades the student begins to focus on particular vocational choices.

A key idea in career education is that people tend to modify or change their interests over time. Career education stresses that this change should be recognized and accommodated naturally within the educational process. Consequently, vocational options should be kept open as much as possible, and training should be designed to develop competencies within occupational clusters rather than being solely targeted at specific jobs. At the junior high level, where course electives typically appear for the first time, this viewpoint suggests that occupational choices should be tentative, and "survey" courses that sample various occupations are preferred to concentrated courses that focus on a specific vocation.

Career Guidance and Counseling

Holland (1974) casts doubt on the argument advanced by many career educators that students will wisely (and correctly) select their lifelong occupation as a result of the assistance they receive in career education classes. He believes that elaborateness in career education is unnecessary and that many individuals will be able to make effective career decisions on their own. While Holland's observation may be true for the non-handicapped, it is questionable that it holds true for the handicapped, for in the absence of career guidance many of them would be apt to choose no career at all. Obviously, such students would never fulfill their personal potential and would end up on welfare rolls.

One of the targets of Holland's criticism has been (in his view) the excessive expense associated with complex, unsystematic career guidance systems. The challenge, then, is to organize career data in a way that makes it readily accessible to individuals for their study and decision making.

A number of comprehensive, computer-based systems have been developed that hold such promise. Some have been developed as an integral part of major instructional innovations such as PLAN*, an individualized curriculum developed by the American Institutes of Research and now marketed by Westinghouse Learning Corporation. Other approaches have focused on computer-based guidance as an independent, personalized search activity. Some career guidance systems have been developed through cooperative multistate consortia.

An example of this latter approach is the subscriber supported EUREKA network, serving secondary school districts, community colleges, state colleges and universities, and educational branches of the armed forces. EUREKA is designed to (a) help users match their preferences, values, and abilities to different occupations and (b) select appropriate programs of training. Some of the questions that can be answered in this computerized information file are as follows:

What are the functions and duties of a particular occupation?
What are the working conditions?
What are the wages and fringe benefits?
What skills and aptitudes are necessary?
Where can a person go to develop the skills and obtain training?
What subjects do you study?
What are the job prospects?
What are the admissions requirements, tuition costs, and financial aid procedures at the various schools?

The EUREKA guidance system just described is the California-wide version of the Career Information System (CIS) developed at the University of Oregon. Evidence of its usefulness lies in the fact that the CIS approach has been adopted for use in over twenty other states.

Occupational Clusters

A number of approaches to occupational clustering have

been developed. Among the better known approaches are (a) the fifteen occupational clusters identified by the United States Office of Education, (b) the grouping identified in the *Dictionary of Occupational Titles,* published by the Department of Labor, and (c) the Project TALENT clusters developed by John Flanagan and his colleagues at the American Institutes for Research, based on a very large scale, longitudinal national sample. Other work classifications include those used by the Census Bureau, with 470 jobs comprising the Industry, Occupational Matrix (IOM), and the *Standard Industrial Classification* (SIC) *Manual* issued by the Bureau of the Budget in 1967. Clustering systems also have been developed at state and local levels to reflect regional variations in employment opportunities.

Each of these clustering approaches has merit in that it offers a highly articulated and coherent means for organizing the world of work and, therefore, for organizing curricular approaches. At the same time, it is true that none of these clustering systems *is in itself* a curriculum, and certainly each must be examined for its utility as far as local job market opportunities are concerned.

The fifteen occupational clusters identified by the United States Office of Education are used quite frequently:

1. Manufacturing
2. Business and Office
3. Marketing and Distribution
4. Personal Service
5. Health
6. Transportation
7. Construction
8. Fine Arts and Humanities
9. Hospitality and Recreation
10. Agri-business and Natural Resources
11. Consumer and Homemaking
12. Communications and Media
13. Public Service
14. Environment
15. Marine Science

Examination of this clustering approach makes clear that mutually exclusive categories are not easily established. Rather, there is a tendency for the clusters to overlap in various ways that can affect the handicapped. As will be explained more fully in a subsequent section, similarities that have to do with the work activities, tools, and materials become significant when job analysis is undertaken preparatory to curriculum building.

The *Dictionary of Occupational Titles* (*DOT*), Third Edition, provides 114 worker trait groups organized within twenty-two general areas as follows:

1. Art
2. Business Relations
3. Clerical Work
4. Counseling, Guidance, and Social Work
5. Crafts
6. Education and Training
7. Elemental Work
8. Engineering
9. Entertainment
10. Farming, Fishing, and Forestry
11. Investigating, Inspecting, and Testing
12. Law and Law Enforcement
13. Machine Work
14. Managerial and Supervisory Work
15. Mathematics and Science
16. Medicine and Health
17. Merchandising
18. Music
19. Personal Service
20. Photography and Communications
21. Transportation
22. Writing

Worker traits are defined in the *DOT* as characteristics required of a worker to achieve average, successful job performance. The six components of worker traits are broken down as follows:

1. Training time
   a. general educational development (reasoning development, mathematical development, and language development)
   b. specific vocational preparation (including type of training and length of training)
2. Aptitudes
   a. intelligence
   b. verbal
   c. numerical
   d. spatial
   e. form perception
   f. clerical perception
   g. motor coordination
   h. manual dexterity
   i. eye-hand-foot coordination
   j. color discrimination
3. Interests
   a. five pairs of interest factors in which alternative types of activities are presented for a forced choice of preference
4. Temperaments
   a. twelve descriptions of situations that are similar to those encountered by workers on the job.
5. Physical demands
   a. lifting, carrying, pushing, pulling (strength)
   b. climbing or balancing
   c. stooping, kneeling, crouching, crawling
   d. reaching, handling, fingering, feeling
   e. talking, hearing
   f. seeing
6. Working conditions
   a. inside, outside, or both
   b. extremes of temperature (hot)
   c. extremes of temperature (cold)
   d. wet and humid
   e. noise and vibrations
   f. hazards
   g. fumes, odors, toxic conditions, dust, poor ventilation

The analysis of Project TALENT data by Flanagan resulted in twelve career groups and 151 specific careers or jobs. The career groups include the following:

1. Engineering, physical sciences, mathematics, architecture (includes 14 careers)
2. Medical, biological sciences (includes 10 careers)
3. Business administration (includes 20 careers)
4. General teaching, social service (includes 23 careers)
5. Humanities: law, social, behavioral sciences (includes 11 careers)
6. Fine arts: performing arts (includes 4 careers)
7. Technical jobs (includes 9 careers)
8. Proprietors, sales workers (includes 11 careers)
9. Mechanics, industrial trades (includes 11 careers)
10. Construction trades (includes 8 careers)
11. Secretarial-clerical office workers (includes 15 careers)
12. General labor: public, community service (includes 15 careers)

Significantly, the longitudinal data from the TALENT study, based on an original sample of 400,000 students, tell a great deal about the interests and abilities of the persons who have filled those kinds of jobs nationally. Thus, Flanagan has developed, in the 1976 *Career Handbook,* comparative "profiles" showing interests of the workers in each of the twelve career clusters. Ten ability scores are also analyzed and comparisons made for each of the 151 job types. A strength of the Flanagan approach to career clustering lies in its visualization of these trait-job relationships. When using the *Career Handbook,* it is a straightforward matter to compare the profile for an individual to the profile that characterizes the overall career group for each of the twelve clusters.

Focusing again on the handicapped, it is appropriate to point out that the Bureau of Education for the Handicapped has had a continuing concern for career development and has sponsored a conference on research needs related to career education for the handicapped in 1975.

A number of recommendations came out of this meeting, including a proposed matrix within which one might approach research in career education of the handicapped (see Figure 1). In addition to its relevance for research strategies, the model represents a helpful balance between living skills and career elements that need to be addressed when curriculum is being planned and training strategies formulated.

In summary, career education has special significance for the handicapped, for they, more than the nonhandicapped, need pre-vocational instruction to adequately prepare them for vocational training, as well as advance planning for the longer term challenge of career advancement once they have proven their worth on the job.

PRE-VOCATIONAL CLASSES

In remarks made at the previously mentioned career education conference on research needs, Melville Appell, Project Officer in career education in the Bureau of Education for the Handicapped, made the observation that "Unfortunately at the present time, 80 percent of the handicapped leaving school in any one year wind up unemployed, dependent on welfare, or under total care." In the face of this grim statistic, it is both natural and necessary that attention should be given to admitting handicapped students to vocational classes *at the earliest time that is consistent with their educational potential.*

Typically, mentally retarded students are more benefited by placement in special vocationally oriented classes where their functional abilities can be developed than they would be if they were placed in classes where academic subject matter is emphasized. At the other extreme, intellectually able students who have the inclination to advance into higher education run a

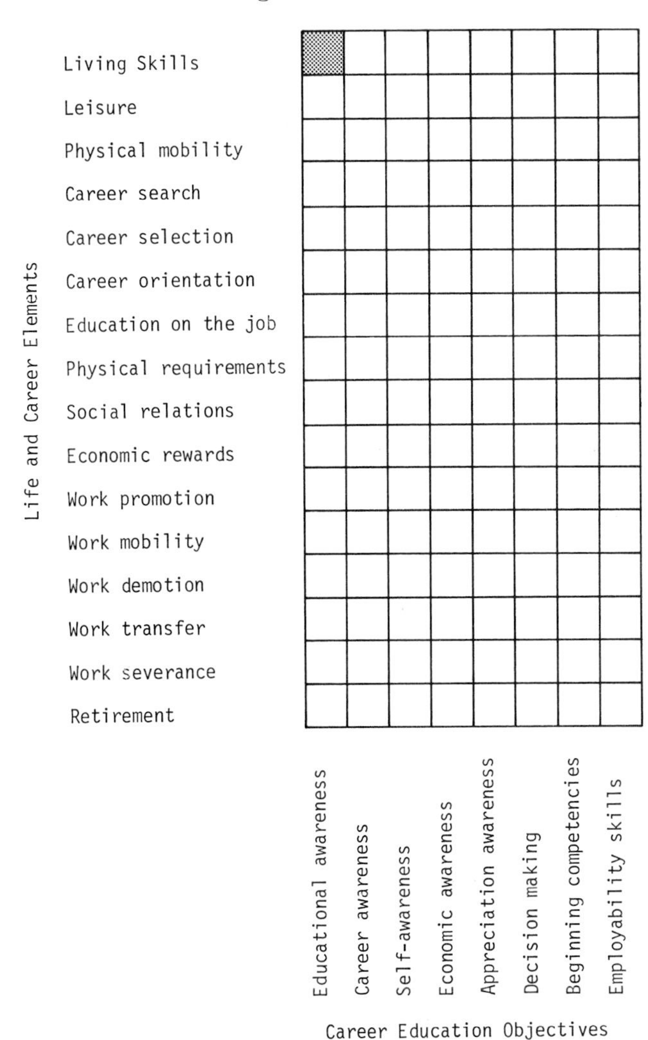

Figure 1. The essential areas of research. Adapted from the Bure: Education for Handicapped: Proceedings of the Conference on Research Related Career Education of the Handicapped, USOE, 1975.

risk of becoming academically prepared but ill equipped to function in work settings. Fortunately, vocational education programs are available at a wide variety of levels and in many forms, allowing handicapped students to gain vocational knowledge and skills that are *appropriate* with regard to their needs.

More than anything else, *pre-vocational instruction* for the handicapped can be thought of as a process of discovery. Typically, it comprises a set of experiences that are designed to

- introduce the student to the processes of self-appraisal and self-help, thereby discovering ways in which he or she can become more self-sufficient and independent;
- help the student to develop important work habits, values, and interpersonal relationships, discovering how his or her own attitudes toward work, work habits, and social interaction on the job can influence job performance;
- acquaint the student with various types of work tasks, discovering what he or she has an interest in doing and can do well.

In essence, these experiences establish the student's abilities and needs in the areas of independent living skills, habits, and attitudes that are work relevant, and mental and motor aspects of task performance.

In addition to these discovery-oriented activities there is an emphasis in most pre-vocational courses on the acquisition of vocational information:

- information about supportive community services (social services, health services, legal services, employment services, rehabilitation services, etc.);
- information about job-finding techniques (want ads, job application forms, interviews, etc.);
- information designed to build job-relevant math and reading skills for payroll deductions, bank accounts, taxes, transportation schedules, business memos, occupational vocabulary, etc.).

The pre-vocational curriculum is usually organized to allow a high degree of individualization in the discovery aspects of the course and a certain amount of group activity for the informational aspects of the course. Instructional materials that are locally available, such as the newspaper, often constitute important resources for the informational aspects of the course. Instructors in pre-vocational classes should (and frequently do) develop a file of locally used job application forms and other sample materials.

Evaluation in Pre-vocational Classes

Since individualization is central to the discovery aspects of the pre-vocational curriculum, it is not surprising that the evaluation of individual differences underlies the processes of self-appraisal, development of work habits and attitudes, and the sampling of work aptitudes and work readiness. (Note: a subsequent chapter in this book will deal in greater detail with testing and the assessment of individual aptitudes and abilities, as well as with various work sampling systems. In this section, we are primarily concerned with the exploratory rather than highly formalized, decision-oriented aspects of vocational evaluation).

As a result of the individual testing that handicapped students undergo as a part of their special education, it is likely that existing test results already give a good indication of the medical, psychological, social, and educational abilities of these students. Building upon these existing data, but applying them to the new priorities of pre-vocational instruction, the special educator and vocational educator should jointly decide whether additional testing is required and what that testing should include. Together, they must keep in mind the restrictions that are associated with the use of (and interpretation of) standardized tests when they are used with special needs students. They also need to be sensitive to any anticipated interaction(s) of the disability with the test administration procedures; that is, there is a possibility of deflated test results due to the nature of the test rather than the student's abilities.

Apart from formalized assessment through testing, pre-vocational evaluation of the student usually involves a considerable amount of observational rating. In the living skills aspects of a pre-vocational course, for example, the evaluation of whether personal grooming is at an acceptable standard derives largely from observational data accumulated over a number of class sessions. Similarly, evidence concerning the individual's ability to follow directions, exercise safety precautions, and function in a socially acceptable manner is typically gained through observation.

As indicated previously, pre-vocational assessment involves the tentative matching of students to occupational fields for which they seem best suited. Since most pre-vocational classes do not entail actual experience on the job (some do involve situational assessment, however), it is appropriate that job elements be simulated as much as possible within the classroom. For example, punctuality on the job can be, and often is, simulated in the classroom by simply adding a time clock, then having the students punch in and out. To encourage these new behaviors, it is essential that there be appropriate acknowledgment of good performance on the part of the handicapped students.

Simulation of job tasks can be relatively straightforward in instances where the tasks are mainly concerned with routine assembly, sorting, or other "routine" activities. In many instances the instructor can obtain a number of the actual parts or items that would be manipulated on the job. These types of tasks can be objectively scored, e.g. accuracy and speed, and generally will be highly predictive of actual job performance. Since pre-vocational classrooms are usually not able to obtain and use costly or complex devices, such as a bank might use for check reconciliation, simpler but similar tasks must be devised. For example, numerical information on checks could be fed into desk-top adding machines to get some idea of the handicapped individual's mathematics and keyboard skills.

To get a complete picture of the student's potential, it is important that a wide range of work samples be provided. To assure that class time is efficiently used, work samples should be analyzed in terms of their similarity to each other and their representation of various occupational clusters. *The Dictionary of Occupational Titles (DOT)* published by the Department of Labor is widely used as a basis for this comparison.

It is important to point out that the work sample rarely equals the job itself, since most jobs are composed of many more job elements than are practical (or necessary) to test. Prevocational assessment and work sample assessment are *not* intended to tell how skillful a person is in a particular job — that must await completion of the training and placement processes. Rather, the use of work samples at the pre-vocational level is intended to focus attention on certain occupational categories in which particular job elements are especially prevalent or critical. Within the range of jobs that are suggested by an occupational cluster, there remain many variations, and the disposition of a student toward an occupational area is by no means a guarantee that *any* job within that occupational area would be highly rewarding. Again, this depends on training options as much as on making an appropriate occupational choice.

PROGRAM VARIATIONS IN VOCATIONAL EDUCATION

Vocational education, like special education, is organized in many different ways depending on a variety of state and local factors. One research study that sought to examine the provision of services for handicapped students in vocational education classes found this diversity to be so extensive as to defy analysis:

> Indeed the variations encountered in the field were so great that it was impossible to synthesize the 92 projects into categories of vocational programming for the handicapped; and in some ways, the overall program defied analysis — statistical or otherwise. (Olympus, 1974, page 114)

In spite of this situation as pertains to the vocational education of the handicapped, it is readily apparent that most vocational education classes were developed to serve regular, nonhandicapped students and only recently have begun serving "mainstreamed" handicapped students.

Vocational Programs for Regular Students

At the secondary level, students generally have the opportunity to select vocational classes at the high school campus, at a regional occupational program, or at a technical training center affiliated with the school system. Occupational education and training are also a strong part of most junior college or community college curricula. In some locales, cooperative arrangements enable secondary level students to participate in these college level classes.

Because of the unique relationship of vocational education to adult living and the earning of income, vocational programs such as regional occupation programs accept enrollments from adults who seek to improve existing job skills or develop different skills needed in a new career. As a consequence, regional occupation programs and other vocational classes may range widely with respect to the ages of the class members. Not only does this mean that instructors must adapt their instruction to individual differences in students' maturity and their awareness of the working world, but it also is apt to have an enriching effect on younger students, helping them to become conscious of the practical significance of their studies in adult terms.

Instructional Areas

As has already been pointed out, there is no single way in which vocational programs are structured at the secondary, postsecondary, and adult levels. In general, vocational courses offered at the lower levels tend to present instructional content at introductory levels. As the mean student age increases, the course content becomes more specific and concentrated.

Of course, instruction can be organized under many different course titles and according to many different occupational groupings or clusters. The classification system given below (California State Department of Education, 1976) serves as an example of one way of organizing the vocational curriculum.

Vocational Area	*Occupational Fields*
Agricultural Education	Plant science; social science; farm management; agricultural mechanics and engineering; and agricultural leadership
Distributive Education	Retailing; wholesaling; manufacturing; storing; transporting; financing.
Office Education	Business data processing; supervision and coordination of office activities; internal and external communication;

	reporting of information.
Home Economics	Care and guidance of children; clothing production, management, and services; housing, home management, and equipment services; institutional management and services; health services in the secondary schools.
Industrial Education	Transportation, communications, construction, manufacturing, fire service, health careers and services, technical crafts, industrial trades
Public Service	School and library services, city, county offices and recreational facilities, housing and urban development, mental health.
Criminal Justice	Law enforcement, corrections, probation and parole, court clerical aide, industrial security, technicians.

While the California state plan gives a general idea of the diversity that exists in the vocational curriculum, it only hints at the tremendous range of courses that are offered in the high schools, the regional occupation programs and centers, and the community colleges. Little would be gained by attempting to list them all here, but it is appropriate to note that the courses range from the generic (metals) to the specific (welding), from the introductory (gardening) to the advanced (horticulture), and from the broadly applied (business machines) to the very narrowly applied (lens grinding). Courses with a more narrow focus, such as the lens grinding class just mentioned, are often organized in response to occupational opportunities in the local labor market. Qualified graduates of these courses frequently find that they have a good opportunity for transition into full-time work if they choose to do so.

This transition is greatly facilitated when the student has had the opportunity to participate in a work experience class, where part of his or her studies are accomplished in actual work situations. California vocational education programs include work experience education of three types:

- Exploratory work experience — There is not intent to

teach productive skills, but rather the intent is to give students the opportunity to systematically observe a variety of occupations.

- General work experience — The principal intent is to give students the opportunity to develop desirable work habits and attitudes while being involved in paid employment.
- Vocational work experience — The central intent is to combine classroom instruction and paid employment experience directly related to each student's occupational goal.

Handicapped students who are mainstreamed in regular vocational classes will, of course, be faced with challenges (both in the school and work contexts) that are not necessarily encountered by nonhandicapped students. Later portions of this book will deal extensively with some of these special problems of adaptation and accommodation to the demands of employment in the community at large.

Vocational Programs for Handicapped Students

The previous brief overview was concerned with vocational classes for regular students as well as "mainstreamed" handicapped persons. Certainly these vocational classes are the ones where the largest number of new problems will be encountered as regular teachers learn to deal effectively with handicapped students within guidelines imposed by recent legislation. In contrast, for a number of years, some vocational classes have been organized specifically to serve the special needs of handicapped students. Included are *sheltered workshops* (typically involving some kind of manufacturing assembly for business firms on a contractual basis), and *work study programs* (courses of study that involve some level of direct employment in the community).

Sheltered workshops, by and large, are not concerned with academic subject matter, nor are they very much concerned with career goals and occupational choices. Rather, the handicapped trainees in sheltered workshops are learning functional job skills and work habits that enable them to generate a modest income. Two examples, from different California communities, may illustrate the range of activities that can be encountered in sheltered workshop vocational training.

The first of these workshops, run as part of a regional occupation program, has been busily engaged in making a variety of products, ranging from "pet rock farms" sold through a large chain of stores serving highway travelers, to heat-formed plastic signs for commercial businesses. The second workshop, operated through a nonprofit community agency, has been sterilizing, repairing, and rebagging passengers' earphones under contract with a major airline and also carrying out various metal stamping and assembly tasks.

Work study programs have been recognized as a practical, effective way to help many students with marginal talents find their way into the working world. Note that work study and work experience are distinguished in this text in that the term *work study* will refer to special classes for the mentally retarded or for other handicapped students whose potential for employment is limited but who are nonetheless able to engage in productive work. *Work experience* will be the term used for regular vocational classes that have an element of community-based work training in occupations related to the vocational course work offered in the school.

As was true with the sheltered workshops, work study programs can vary a great deal in how they are organized and what work skills are learned. One very successful work study program, operated by a school district in southern California, has a work study agreement with a large motel affiliated with one of the nation's largest chains. In this program a group of educable mentally retarded students has been assigned helper "jobs" at the motel including food preparation, food service, housekeeping, laundry and linen service, office and front desk service, and bellhop and elevator service. In another work study program, elsewhere in southern California, arrangements have been made to have students assist in the care of grounds and facilities under control of the city parks and recreation department.

In neither of these locations was it assured that students would be employed on a continuing basis following the work study experience. Nevertheless, some students are placed in this manner, and work placement for the others is certainly facilitated.

On the instructional side, the techniques developed by instructors in these segregated vocational training contexts have relevance for regular vocational educators as well as for special educators, as they jointly attempt to modify regular vocational programming to meet the special needs of handicapped persons. For example, by breaking down instruction into small steps (considerably smaller than would normally be the case), instructors have found that the mentally retarded can learn a surprisingly wide variety of vocational skills, including some in which the complexities involved (such as in motorcycle repair) are considerable. Clearly, what works for more seriously handicapped students should also be helpful to others, less severely handicapped, who are enrolled in regular vocational classes.

Specialized Noneducational Training Programs

Vocational training is carried out by a variety of agencies *not* directly affiliated with public education though perhaps cooperating with them in some way. Earlier it was pointed out that cooperation with the Department of Rehabilitation has been very beneficial to some school programs. This cooperation has generally tended to take the form of specialized support, such as counseling or transportation. Indirectly, the long-term *experience* of the Department of Rehabilitation in providing for vocational training of handicapped adults can be a source of valuable insights for the planning of vocational instruction of students at the secondary and community college levels.

In this latter regard a useful parallel can be drawn between the Individualized Educational Program (IEP) mandated for each handicapped student in the schools and the Individualized Written Rehabilitation Program (IWRP) required for each handicapped person served by the Department of Rehabilitation. An interesting and important aspect of the IWRP, which vocational educators and special educators can both appreciate, involves its three implicit phases or levels of service. Expressed in client terms, the first level consists of "extended evaluation services," which basically involves a trial period of exploratory vocational assessment prior to making firm decisions about vocational goals. Within the schools, this level of client service roughly parallels the offering of pre-vocational courses and career education activities, especially those consisting of short miniclasses in which students are exposed to different vocational areas.

As the second level of IWRP service is reached, the individual client is given specific training aimed at preparing that person for a chosen occupational field or, more likely, for a specific job. In the school context this service level is paralleled by specialized vocational classes, e.g. horticulture or floristry, and by training in work experience settings, e.g. a nursery or a retail store.

At the third level, the IWRP provides for the possibility of follow-up supportive services *after* the individual has been placed on the job. This is particularly logical because initial placement in a job is neither an assurance of success in the job nor an indication of satisfaction with the job.

It is this latter level of the IWRP service sequence that may be especially informative to vocational educators and special educators as they plan the IEP for handicapped students. Historically, and for reasons that stem largely from the concept of "graduation" and the consequent limits of school authority, there has been all too little follow-up of vocational graduates. There has been relatively little effort expended in an attempt to ascertain their work status and virtually no effort to provide help or supportive instruction once the handicapped person has become employed. This apparent lack is partially justified on the grounds that the graduate is probably eligible to become a rehabilitation client and receive appropriate services. This justification, of course, is dependent upon a high degree of coordination and communication between the education and rehabilitation professional staffs, which unfortunately does not always occur.

What, then, can be extrapolated from the IWRP follow-up and applied to school-based vocational education and the planning of IEPs for handicapped students? First, without some measure of follow-up it is difficult (if not impossible) to assess the *outcomes* of vocational instruction for handicapped students or to make appropriate *revisions* in future course content to better prepare the trainees. Second, to the extent that schools can keep in touch with handicapped graduates from their vocational programs and learn of the progress they are making, this information can be inspirational to other handicapped students still in the program and still looking hopefully toward a satisfying, productive career.

In review, this chapter has given a brief overview of the ways in which pre-vocational and vocational courses are organized. In general, this organization has come about without special consideration for the handicapped, who only recently have gained access to the broad range of vocational offerings. Although a number of handicapped students are now participating in "mainstream" vocational education, others are best served through specialized courses geared to their functional abilities. Through a combination of career education, prevocational coursework and evaluation, exploratory vocational classes, specialized training, and work experience in the community, it is now possible for every handicapped student to discover and realize his or her vocational potential.

PART II

THE SPECIAL EDUCATION/VOCATIONAL EDUCATION TEAM AND THE PROVISION OF APPROPRIATE EDUCATIONAL SERVICES

CHAPTER 4

THE SPECIAL EDUCATION/VOCATIONAL EDUCATION TEAM AND THE REALIZATION OF INDIVIDUAL POTENTIAL

THE unique circumstances encountered when a particular handicapped person enters a program of vocational education present a challenge to the professional staff. It is not possible to ignore this challenge, since both P.L. 94-142 and P.L. 94-482 specifically require the staff to provide *appropriate* educational experiences commensurate with the *individual* student's potential. This being the case, and recognizing that this challenge places requirements upon the vocational educator that may well exceed his or her capabilities, the special educator has an opportunity and a responsibility to function in a *team relationship* with that vocational educator to the benefit of the handicapped student.

Since the special educator and the vocational educator each have important information to share, they should communicate freely and meet as frequently as necessary to plan instruction in accordance with the particular student's needs. Their interaction and cooperation will be dependent, of course, on the previous experience each has had in similar situations and on the specific circumstances surrounding each individual student's case.

The special educator/vocational educator team can be mutually reinforcing at a number of specific points during the handicapped student's vocational training. In many respects these points are part of *overall individual educational program development and implementation.*

Among the most important are

- appraisal of needs and assessment of capabilities and preferences;

- planning of appropriate curricula and implementation of instruction;
- overcoming barriers, including those related to attitudes, communication, accessibility, and transportation;
- facilitating the transition from vocational instruction to daily living applications.

Two earlier texts by staff of the American Institutes for Research give a number of suggestions, illustrations, and examples of use to vocational educators as they become involved in these four major activities. These texts are *Vocational Education: Teaching the Handicapped in Regular Classes,* by Robert Weisgerber et al., published by the Council for Exceptional Children, Reston, Virginia, 1978, and *Mainstreaming Guidebook for Vocational Educators Teaching the Handicapped,* by Peter Dahl, Judith Appleby, and Dewey Lipe, published by Olympus Publishing Company, Salt Lake City, 1978.

While it preceded these by several years, another exceptionally useful resource guide, and one with which the present volume is in close agreement, is *Instructional Development for Special Needs Learners: An Inservice Resource Guide,* by L. Allen Phelps, published by the University of Illinois at Urbana-Champaign, 1976.

Each of these three earlier volumes stemmed from grants from the Office of Education; the first and third from the Bureau of Occupational and Adult Education, and the second from the Bureau of Education for the Handicapped. This mutuality of interest in vocational education for the handicapped at the federal level reinforces the fundamental principle that the challenge is not "assignable" but is a shared responsibility at the local level.

EVALUATION FOR DECISION MAKING

Earlier, the appropriateness of the education being provided to the handicapped student was emphasized. Clearly, the instructional process is spread out over time and involves many steps or stages. To state that an instructional program is appropriate to the student, then, it is necessary to establish that fact on a continuing basis throughout the overall instructional process.

The use of systematic evaluation of one form or another is important to the whole process, for it makes possible informed decision making at each stage of planning, instructing, and placing students. Figure 2 is intended to show the stages or progressions from the intake of the student to the placement of the student in a paying job and makes clear the relationship of evaluation and decision making at each stage. Although the explanations in Figure 2 are brief, it is possible to see that decision making in the absence of evaluative evidence at any stage is highly undesirable. Accordingly, the balance of this section of the book will concentrate on the ways in which the

	(multistage) EVALUATION	(leads to) FINDINGS	(resulting in) DECISIONS
Stage 1	IEP assessment and learner profile	Specifies areas of student's strengths and needs	Recommendation for educational assignment and short/and long-term goals for the individual
Stage 2	Vocational assessment and learner profile	Identifies student's existing performance skills, interests, work readiness, etc.	Recommendation for various occupations that are promising for the individual
Stage 3	Job market analysis and community profile	Establishes number and type of jobs open or anticipated	Recommendations for course offerings and the feasible level of enrollment
Stage 4	Task analysis and job requirements profile	Establishes employer expectations and priorities on the job	Recommendation for course content and relative emphasis in accordance with handicapped individual's abilities
Stage 5	Acquired competencies and learner profile	Establishes the key outcomes of training and job readiness	Recommendations for further study or for work placement during or at the end of the training period
Stage 6	Employment profile for learner	Establishes student's performance while on the job	Recommendations for advanced training, indefinite placement, or eligibility for employment

Figure 2. The importance of evaluation for decision making at various stages of planning, instruction, and placement.

special education staff can work cooperatively with the vocational education staff to apply evaluative procedures at each stage of planning, instruction, and placement. Throughout, heavy emphasis will be given to the use of forms already in use or recommended for use in the field. Fictitious student cases will be given to illustrate the use of the forms and to draw out principles that are especially important to keep in mind when planning vocational education for students having different types of handicaps.

CHAPTER 5

APPRAISAL OF NEEDS AND ASSESSMENT OF CAPABILITIES AND PREFERENCES

A CENTRAL idea throughout this book is the necessity of recognizing individual differences and forming instructional strategies that reflect those differences in meaningful, constructive ways. To a large extent this sensitivity to individual differences is empathetic and ongoing. That is, the teacher often learns heuristically how best to work with a child to achieve desired results, and what can be set as reasonable goals. While this informal interaction between teacher and student is an important part of any vocational program, and is to be encouraged, it is also true that formalized assessment can aid substantially in identification of those individual differences that bear importantly on future vocational success and, therefore, should be reflected in the instructional programming for the individuals involved.

Assessment can be viewed as a way of systematically gathering information about individuals to make informed judgments about their readiness, needs, and accomplishments. Assessment does not automatically imply testing, though it is unlikely that assessment could be viewed as complete in the absence of any testing, be it psychological, academic, or of some other type.

There is extraordinary diversity encountered in the handicapped population, both in terms of the type of disabling condition and the level of severity of that condition. When this diversity is combined with the general variabilities that characterize the human race as a whole, such as variations in experience, interest, aptitude, ability, and maturity, it is understandable that the evaluation of handicapped persons' readiness, needs, and accomplishments should be done selectively in the light of its *appropriateness and applicability* for each person, and not administered simply because of programmatic routine. Thus, if the reason for the assessment is not established, and the use to which findings can be put is not clear or mandated by law, then there is not a great deal of merit to gathering that information.

In the light of this practical orientation to assessment, it must be remembered that nothing in the preceding statement suggests that assessment can be dispensed with, and it should not be used in a perfunctory manner simply to comply with externally imposed requirements. Rather, it should be approached as a vital and natural part of the overall instructional planning, monitoring, and evaluation process for each handicapped student.

If vocational instruction for the handicapped is to be made relevant to the needs of the individual, there are a number of relationships that should be understood in the overall assessment-design-instruction-work placement continuum. Figure 3 gives a schematic representation of the major elements to be considered. Each of these elements will be discussed in some detail later in this section, but for the moment merely note that the IEP assessment precedes and (in effect) supersedes vocational assessment. That is, the IEP must call for vocational involvement before any vocational assessment is germane and useful. Paralleling this assessment of the individual is the assessment of the job market, hopefully with some regularity, by the vocational education staff. If a job market exists in an occupational area, and the course is to reflect that job market, it is appropriate to carry out task analysis procedures so that individual differences can be "matched" to job requirements. As shown in Figure 3, course design derives largely from the IEP and job market combination. Thus, the instructional assignment of a handicapped student typically is a reflection of an IEP decision, while the offering of the course within the school's instructional program should reflect job opportunities for those who enroll.

Individual instruction, as shown in Figure 3, involves a modification of the course design to suit the individual's needs. Together, the combination of course design and individual instruction is what will qualify the person for some kind of work opportunity that could range from work study or work

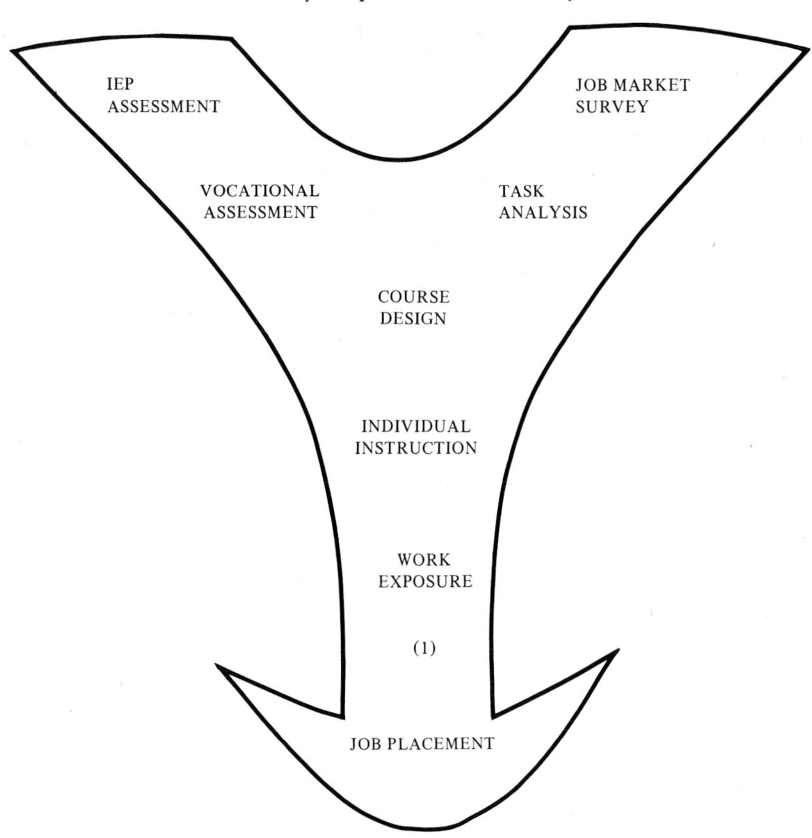

(1) Alternatively, this could lead to advanced study in preparation for a career goal.

Figure 3. A schematic representation of the assessment, design, instruction, and work placement continuum.

experience programs to a variety of part-time or full-time job placements.

USING THE IEP AS A PLANNING TOOL

The classification of a student as being handicapped and, therefore, deserving of special education services, is a process that occurs apart from and antecedent to the involvement of that student in vocational classes. For that reason, a fund of information is usually already available that can have practical impact on the design of vocational planning and instruction.

By law, the IEP contains certain types of information that serve to (1) identify the student, (2) summarize test results and observational evidence that are used in deciding on appropriate placement, (3) characterize the student's strengths and weaknesses on a general level, (4) identify certain needs that can be addressed through educational programming, (5) specify who is to deliver these educational services and what media, resources, or other support may be required, (6) establish major goals and objectives, (7) provide for periodic review of accomplishments, and (8) document the agreement of the IEP team members (including the parent and possibly the student) as to the content in the IEP, as evidenced by the signatures of those persons involved.

An example of an IEP as adapted from the San Diego school district is shown in Figure 4. Although the IEP shown here covers a range of topics and is several pages long, it nevertheless serves mainly as a tool for facilitating decisions about placement in the "least restrictive environment" and as a means for defining what an "appropriate" education would be for that student. It should be noted, at this point, that the IEP format in Figure 4 is not being recommended as a model but rather as an illustration of the information that such a document often contains. As is well known to special education professionals, considerable variation exists in the format of IEPs used by local school districts.

Staff in the San Mateo (CA) Unified School District, as in many districts, are very much aware of the need to follow through on each of the prescriptive elements contained in any IEP. Accordingly, they supplement the IEP with an additional form, which they refer to as the Individualized Instructional Plan (IIP). An important distinction between the IEP and the IIP is that the latter is to be completed by the receiving teacher, the person who has been assigned responsibility for implementing the IEP. This receiving person can, and often will, be a vocational educator as placement teams at the secondary level become more familiar with new options open to the student under the vocational education umbrella.

I. STUDENT IDENTIFICATION

Name ______ Sex M ___ F ___ I.D.# ______

Birthdate ______ C.A. ___ Grade ___ Kdgn Entry Date ______

School ______ Teacher ______

Parents ______

Address ______ Phone ______

District of Residence ______

Primary Language of:

Home ______ Pupil ______ How Determined ______

II. ASSESSMENT INFORMATION

Indicate Present Levels of Student Performance if Applicable

Based on: Developmental Summary ______ Speech and Language Report ______

Psycho-educational Reports ______ Physician's Report (as needed) ______

Academic Achievement: ______

Communication Development: ______

Figure 4. Individualized Education Program (IEP) (page 1).

Social Adaptation: ______________________________

____

____

____

____

Pre-vocational and Vocational: ______________________________

____

____

____

____

Psychomotor: ______________________________

____

____

____

____

Self-Help Skills: ______________________________

____

____

____

____

III. PROGRAM INFORMATION

____

Special Education

Program ______________ Date of Enrollment ______________

Projected Duration ______________ Special Teacher ______________

Rationale for Placement (least restrictive concept) ______________

____

____

____

Figure 4. Individualized Education Program (IEP) (page 2).

Services to be Provided to Regular Teacher ______________________

____

P.E. Program ______________ Prevocational ____________

Vocational ______________________________________

Additional Support Services ______________________

(Specify Date of Initiation and Duration

and Personnel Responsible) ______________________

____

____

____

____

IV. IMPLEMENTATION INFORMATION

Learning Styles:

Rate ____

Modality ____

____

Learning Situation:

Time ____

Interaction ______________________________________

____

Place, Materials, etc. ____________________________

____

____

Student Interests, Talents, etc. ____________________

____

____

Behavior Strengths: ______________________________

____

____

Figure 4. Individualized Education Program (IEP) (page 3).

Effective Reinforcers: ____________________

____

____

____

Special Instructional Media and Materials: ____________________

____

____

____

Personnel Responsible for Implementation of IEP: ____________________

____

V. MEETING INFORMATION

____

IEP Meeting Date ________ Interpreter Required: Yes ______ No ________

____________________ ____________________

(Parent Signature) (Administrator Signature)

Attended Meeting: Yes _____ No _____ ____________________

(Specialist/Teacher Signature)

____________________ ____________________

(Pupil Signature) (Other: position)

____

(Other: position)

____

Figure 4. Individualized Education Program (IEP) (page 4).

VI. PRIORITIZED LONG RANGE GOALS

AND PERIODIC OBJECTIVES Student Name ______________________

LONG RANGE GOAL ______________	MONITORING GOALS AND OBJECTIVES
Periodic Objective(s) ______________	______________
(Specify time, observable behavior, evaluation conditions, and criteria.)	Date: ______________
	Achieved ______________
______________	Reviewed ______________
______________	Revision Recommended ______________
______________	
______________	
______________	
Person Responsible ______________	
Date Established ______________	

LONG RANGE GOAL ______________	MONITORING GOALS AND OBJECTIVES
Periodic Objective(s) ______________	______________
(Specify time, observable behavior, evaluation conditions, and criteria.)	Date: ______________
	Achieved ______________
______________	Reviewed ______________
______________	Revision Recommended ______________
______________	
______________	
______________	
______________	
Person Responsible ______________	
Date Established ______________	

Figure 4. Individualized Education Program (IEP) (page 5).

VII. SHORT TERM OBJECTIVES

INDIVIDUAL INSTRUCTIONAL PLAN

To be completed by personnel responsible for implementation.

DISTRICT/SCHOOL ____ STUDENT'S NAME __________ C.A. ___ DATE ____

LONG RANGE GOAL ______________________________

PERIODIC OBJECTIVE ______________________________

____

____

____

____

LEARNING STYLE ______________________________

____

BEHAVIORAL STRENGTHS ______________________________

____

SHORT TERM OBJECTIVES (Section 3153 Title V Regulations 5-22-77)	INTERVENTION ACTIVITIES AND MATERIALS	MONITORING OF OBJECTIVES
______	______	Person or persons responsible for implementation
______	______	______
______	______	______
______	______	______
______	______	Reviewed ______
______	______	Date ______
______	______	Achieved ______
______	______	Date ______
______	______	Revision
______	______	recommended ______

Figure 4. Individualized Education Program (IEP) (page 6).

The usefulness of an IIP to supplement and build on the IEP becomes apparent when a handicapped student is assigned to a vocational class because the IEP *must* be supplemented with a substantial amount of vocationally relevant information if the receiving vocational education staff are to provide the appropriate education that is called for in the law. Research presently underway (under the sponsorship of the Bureau of Occupational and Adult Education, USOE) is aimed at developing IEP procedures that are specific to vocational education. As a part of this effort, in its later stages, dissemination is planned to state staffs and subsequently to local staffs through a workshop strategy. Presumably, then, there should be a trend toward the standardization of vocationally oriented IEPs over the next two or three years.

Hopefully, the involvement of vocational educators in the IEP process itself will become much more commonplace, as is the case in Massachusetts, where Regulation 766 (September, 1978) defines the membership of the evaluation TEAM to include

> . . . an approved vocational educator, if the TEAM intends to make a vocational education prescription for the child; provided that if the TEAM is considering recommending a placement in a vocational technical high school the vocational technical school director or designee shall attend the meeting.

In its present form, what can the IEP "say" to the vocational educator? To answer this question, selected elements of the sample IEP in Figure 4 will be examined as though it were filled out for a fictitious student. Specifically, we would like to establish what might be helpful to course planning.

In this case, the student is Monty, a visually handicapped fifteen year old who is also paralyzed from the waist down. The list below summarizes some of the entered statements along with possible implications for the vocational classroom.

SUMMARY OF IEP FOR MONTY	*VOCATIONAL EDUCATION IMPLICATIONS*
Academic: Standardized test results are at grade level (plus or minus one grade)	Intellectually, Monty should be able to understand and deal with the difficulty level in course materials.

Communication: Verbally fluent, but listens only when motivated. Uses braille.	Monty should be able to communicate orally with his instructor and classmates but may need to be checked (through teacher questioning or other means) to be sure that attention was given to specific task instructions. Brailling of lesson material is appropriate.
Social adaptation: Uses attention-getting techniques, good sense of humor, critical of others.	Dealing with Monty in class may call for tact and diplomacy. For example, he should not monopolize the classroom discussions or ask questions needlessly. Be alert to possible problems in using the "buddy" system.
Pre-vocational and Vocational: No existing assessment data, generally limited in his knowledge of vocational options.	Career awareness, vocational work sample assessments, and other preliminary steps (such as a "survey" course or visits to community businesses) are advisable.
Psychomotor: Wheelchair bound; weak hands but coordination good; vision level so poor that eye/hand coordination is not relevant.	Facilities will have to be checked both for access (building, room, work station, tools) and for hazards. Mobility may be a problem. Task adaptation and special instructional techniques will be required. Additional testing is needed to establish his useful level of vision.
Self-help skills: Presentable in appearance; needs help in elimination.	Monty's appearance is a sign of good personal habits that can be important in many jobs. Further information should be obtained about teacher responsibilities and procedures for assistance when Monty needs to go to the restroom.
Program Information: Name of special education teacher; types of instructional or consultation support available; special equipment or resources available.	Persons to be contacted and special equipment, etc. that can facilitate instruction.
Implementation Information: Preferred learning style is tactile-Kinesthetic; in learning situation tires after 20 minutes on task, and works best in tutorial context, seating placement that assures good	Monty should be given chances to "feel" his work unless unsafe. Give him "breaks" or otherwise provide relaxation, seat him near the front where he can be guided in tasks as needed. Build on Monty's recall,

hearing and access to materials; interests are mostly centered on intellectual activities and games; one behavior strength is recall, another is his problem-solving ability; reinforcers include positive statements and acknowledgement of his work; special media include some beginning use of the Optacon (ink print reading device.)	but also involve him in deductive/analytic processes relating to course content. Praise him for work that is done well and in timely fashion. Explore the use of the Optacon for some instructional materials, but do not depend on it because of his slower reading rate.
Meeting Information: Lists persons present when IEP was discussed.	May suggest the extent to which Monty's parents and other teachers are informed and possibly could assist in some way as questions arise.
Long-Range Goals and Periodic Objectives: General goal is to explore vocational areas that would be helpful to a career, for example, in developing typing skills, leading to improved academic communication, furtherance of his verbal fluency, and possible connection to journalistic or other intellectual/verbal vocations.	Suggests curricular emphasis as well as the types of careers in which work experience placement might be considered for Monty. Ways should be found to connect vocational classwork with broader applications.
Short Term Objectives: In the next 6-8 weeks additional work-related evaluation should be accomplished, and survey visits made to community businesses.	Pre-vocational activities, rather than specific skill development, should be emphasized at first so that Monty can participate in an informed, intelligent way in shaping his own career decisions and vocational training.

Many of the IEP implications for vocational planning as pointed out above would be apparent to a thoughtful, experienced vocational educator. The special educator, however, should offer any *additional insights* that can be gained through a more detailed examination of the diagnostic test data that must (by law) have been available at the time of the IEP meeting. It is not reasonable to expect the vocational educator to be well grounded in diagnostic testing and, therefore, able to do his or her own interpretive analysis of the student's test results. It would be helpful if the test data could be displayed (and then described) in the form of a learning profile. Figure 5 shows an example of such an approach for a different student, one who had been tested with the WISC, ITPA, and the Frostig. The results are integrated in a way that allows strengths and weaknesses to be profiled and compared.

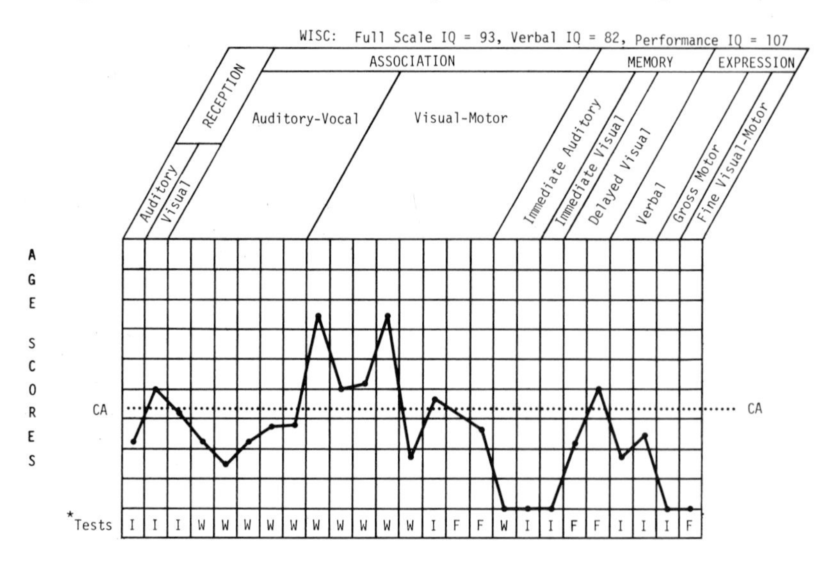

Figure 5. A learning profile for test data. From Eleanore T. Kenney: Learning disability: What it is and is not. *Educational Leadership, 32(8):* 507-510, May, 1975. Adapted with permission of the Association for Supervision and Curriculum Development, and Eleanore T. Kenney. Copyright © 1975 by the Association for Supervision and Curriculum Development. All rights reserved.

By using a display format such as that shown in Figure 5 (adapted as necessary for the tests involved) the special educator can point out selected learning patterns that could have ramifications for instructional design. In the case illustrated in Figure 5, memory and expression scores tend to be low, especially the immediate auditory memory and immediate visual memory scores. Gross motor and fine visual-motor expression are low as well. When this is contrasted with high visual-motor association scores, the discrepancy spans six age equivalents. Based on this information, the role the special educator should then play is one of helping the vocational educator to develop techniques for taking full advantage of the student's strengths, while at the same time providing positive reinforcement and support in the student's areas of weakness. It is very important not to *overreact* to test results in terms of student placement. For example, Johnson (1973) has cited several examples of faulty placement based on extremely low audiogram evaluations while ignoring other compensating factors.

Phelps (1976) has developed another approach to displaying a variety of test results in a learner analysis profile. Rather than organizing the profile by test categories, he has chosen to organize it by skills categories and directly labels the five-point rating scale as learning difficulty to learning strength (rather than using age or grade equivalent scores). Figure 6 shows an example of Phelp's format, filled out for Buck, a fictitious deaf student.

Phelps stresses that the profile entries should be based on documented evidence. This can include the following:

- Teacher report/referral
- Diagnostic-prescriptive assessment
- Social service agency referral
- Parent communication
- Employer/supervisor communication
- Work sample evaluation report/profile
- Medical examination
- School achievement/attendance records
- Visual or hearing exam

As can be seen in Figure 6, this approach has several advantages. First, it allows quick scanning and easy comparisons; second, the skills categories have clear significance for vocational applications; third, it adds anecdotal information (observed behaviors), which can pinpoint particular learning problems or strengths.

In Buck's case, as with many deaf students, verbal communication (intelligibility of speech) is poor, his language skills tend to be low, with a weakness in vocabulary, and his sociability represents an area of difficulty. Developing these areas of weakness to a more effective level should be a high priority for Buck if he intends to capitalize on the high potential he shows in quantitive/numerical, cognitive, perceptual, and psychomotor skills areas. In other words, Buck's instructional program should include substantial cooperation between the special educator (for improved speech production) and the vocational educator (for vocabulary lists, opportunities to com-

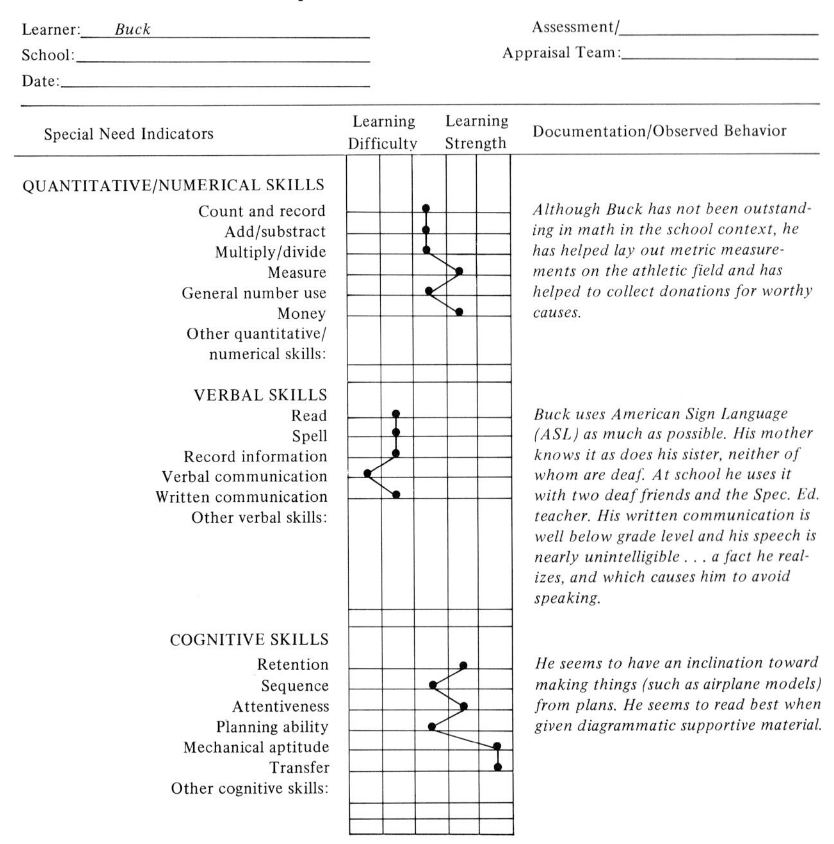

Figure 6. Learner analysis profile (page 1).

municate in class, etc.). Without such a focused effort, Buck's career options will be limited, both in the types of work he could do and in the extent to which he could expect to move up the career ladder in any occupational field he chooses.

Once the decision has been reached concerning the extent to which the student can benefit from being mainstreamed, or the instructional environment that is "least restrictive," it becomes appropriate to establish the proper selection of courses for that student, reflecting his or her knowledge, interests, aptitudes, and experience. It is at this point that vocational evaluation becomes highly important.

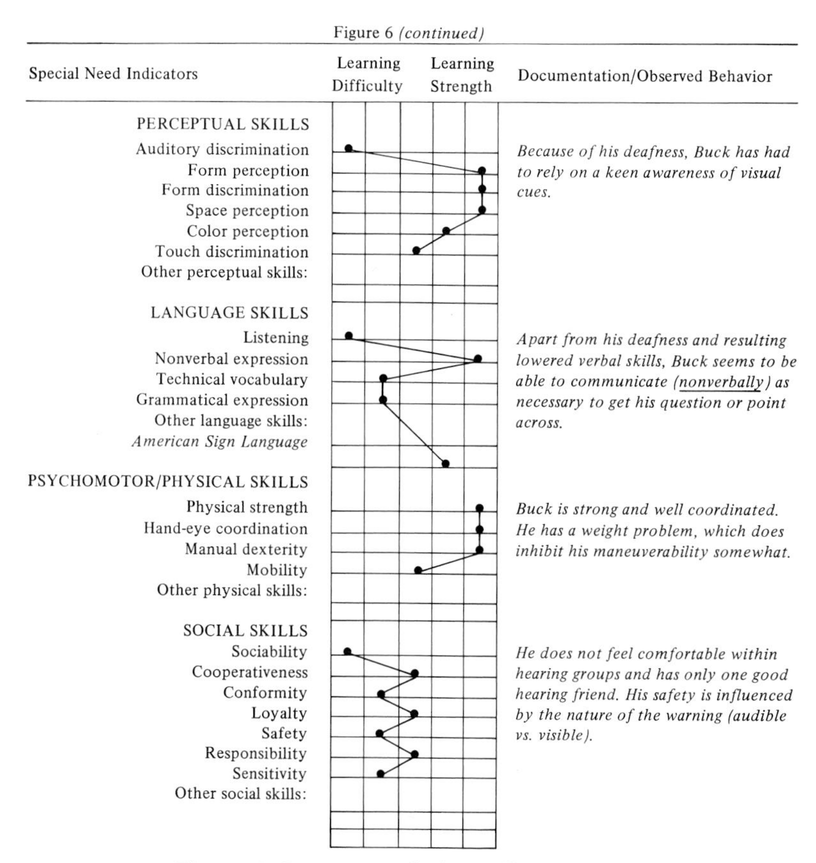

Figure 6. Learner analysis profile (page 2).

VOCATIONAL ASSESSMENT AS A PLANNING TOOL

For many handicapped students the first contact with vocational education will consist of a *pre-vocational* course. Many other students will first undergo *vocational evaluation* to help place them in vocational courses that reflect their interests, abilities, and level of maturity. Sometimes the two activities are combined. The assignment of a handicapped student directly into a vocational training program without preliminary assessments of any form is not really fair to the student or, for that manner, to the instructional staff. Such a "shortcut" would be analagous to making IEP decisions without the benefit of test data or prior knowledge of the student's performance, and that certainly is not an advisable procedure. It follows, then, that either or both of these activities should occur *early* in the student's secondary education rather than late, as too often has been the case.

Using Career Education Information

Hopefully, the student has had prior exposure to career education concepts in previous classes and has developed preliminary understanding about our work-oriented society and about the variety of occupational choices that is possible. To the extent that there has been involvement in career education it is possible that the student has already indicated some preference for a particular type of occupation. In turn, such a preference suggests a logical assignment to a vocational skills class, if the institution offers training in the area of the student's interest.

In addition to any information stemming from career education involvement, it is appropriate to evaluate the student's aptitudes, and interests, career maturity, and work values.

The special educator should realize that vocational evaluation has many facets. It can be accomplished through a study program or a systematic testing program, a work sample evaluation strategy, a behavioral observation approach, or some combination of these. Shigley (1976) has described vocational evaluation as a process of medical, psychological, social, vocational, educational, cultural, and economic evaluation. This, of course, is a comprehensive definition and in some respects idealistic. That is, not all vocational decision making needs to be dependent upon such a totality of information as this definition would seem to suggest. Within his defined framework, Shigley points out that emphasis is given to assessment that uses work, real or simulated, as the focal point of the evaluation.

Using Test Information

It is beyond the scope of this chapter to list and comment on the wide variety of aptitude tests, interest inventories, and special purpose career and vocational assessment tools that are available. For this, the reader is referred to a comprehensive comparison and description of various measurement instruments available in the *Handbook of Measurement and Evaluation in Rehabilitation*, edited by Brian Bolton and published in 1976. The chapter entitled "Vocational Inventories," written by Lenore Harmon, ViJay Sharma and Ann Trotter, is quite helpful in selecting appropriate measures of interests and career maturity. The authors have included descriptions of some twenty-two measures along with appraisals of their purpose, reliability, and validity. Criteria for their use with special populations are given, as are appraisals of their readability, expressed in grade level equivalents. Similarly, the chapter entitled "Aptitude and Achievement Tests," by Randall Parker and Carl Hansen, is useful in comparing the various aptitude tests and in relating eight occupational groups to the testing of intellectual abilities, spatial and mechanical abilities, perceptual accuracy, motor abilities, and personality traits.

In the same volume the comprehensive General Aptitude Test Battery (GATB) is described in detail by Robert Droege and Hendrik Mugass, including its application with deaf persons, mentally retarded persons, and the educationally deficient. Developed by the United States Employment Service (USES), the battery has usefulness not only in public employment interviewing but also can be used in other contexts that are nonprofit in nature when the situation warrants.

While the GATB is a battery designed to measure abilities, it is seen as just one of a number of useful measures identified by René Dawis, author of the chapter entitled "The Minnesota Theory of Work Adjustments." In addition to the GATB, the theory embraces the following:

- The Minnesota Satisfaction Questionnaire (MSQ), to measure satisfaction with various job aspects such as responsibility, advancement and recognition;
- The Minnesota Importance Questionnaire (MIQ), to measure the individual's subjective needs such as the "ideal" job;
- The Minnesota Job Description Questionnaire (MJDQ), to describe various job reinforcers important to the individual;

- The Minnesota Satisfactoriness Scales (MSS), to measure performance, conformance, dependability, and personal adjustment;
- The Occupational Reinforcer Patterns (ORP), which corresponds with the MIQ and is used for profiling and prediction purposes;
- The Occupational Aptitude Patterns (OAP), which relates to the GATB and is used for prediction of the correspondence between an individual's abilities with the requirements of specific work environments.

As has been indicated previously, it is essential that the assessment of handicapped persons be undertaken in a manner that reflects an intelligent consideration of the *possible interactions between the handicapping condition and the measure* being used. This point is established convincingly by Mary Bauman, by Edna Levine, and by Marvin Rosen and Marvin Kivitz, who respectively have contributed chapters in the *Handbook of Measurement and Evaluation in Rehabilitation* on the psychological evaluation of the blind client, the deaf client, and the mentally retarded client. Each chapter fully treats the special problems encountered and makes concrete suggestions about various approaches and measures that can be used.

The selection of appropriate vocational tests may seem difficult and time-consuming, with little assurance that the tests selected are going to provide the type of standardized information that lends itself to meaningful analysis and comparison. In that regard it may be helpful to become familiar with the reference tool *Vocational Tests and Reviews,* edited by Oscar Krisen Buros. The 1,114 pages in the 1975 edition, for example, present 649 vocational tests (429 in print), 675 test reviews, 6,652 references to these tests in the literature, a cumulative name index for each test, a directory of publishers, as well as author and title indexes.

The following brief list is included to illustrate the variety of vocational tests available. It is neither meant as a recommendation of these particular measures nor as a complete or balanced battery.

VOCATIONAL INTERESTS AND APTITUDES

Comprehensive Career Assessment Scale — Designed to determine the interest and familiarity an individual has with various types of careers and job clusters at two levels (grades 3-7 and grades 8-12).

COPS (California Occupational Preference Survey) — Designed to compare relative strengths and interests of various occupational activities of adolescents and adults.

JOB-O — Enables the student to choose and compare information about jobs of interest out of 120 jobs correlated to the United States Department of Labor Occupational Classifications and Occupational Outlook Handbook.

San Francisco Vocational Competency Scale — The purpose of this inventory is to measure the vocational competency of individuals 18 years or older whose primary disability is mental retardation.

VISA (Vocational Interest and Sophistication Assessment) — Reading-free picture test designed to determine the interest pattern and knowledge of mildly retarded adolescents and young adults for selected job categories.

D.A.T. (Differential Aptitude Tests) — An integrated battery of aptitude tests designed for educational and vocational guidance. The D.A.T. provides a profile of relative strengths and weaknesses of students in the following eight abilities: Verbal Reasoning, Numerical Ability, Abstract Reasoning, Space Relations, Mechanical Reasoning, Clerical Speed and Accuracy, Spelling and Language Usage.

Diagnostic Reading Scales (Spache) — Tests word recognition, reading comprehension on individuals in independent, instructional and potential levels as well as a supplementary phonic test for normal and retarded readers at elementary school levels and retarded readers in junior and senior high school age groups.

Minnesota Rate of Manipulation — Measures manual dexterity for job placement in five areas: placing, turning, displacing, one-hand turning and placing, and two-hand turning and placing.

Pennsylvania Bi-Manual Worksample — This test combines

sub-tests in finger dexterity, gross movements of arms, eye-hand coordination, and bi-manual coordination to measure the individual's ability to use hands in cooperation.

Using Job Sampling

Apart from the large array of tests that is already available for establishing vocational readiness, it should be kept in mind that pre-vocational assessment typically will involve some combination of job sampling or job exploration. These may be carried out as short-term, i.e. two-week, work sample evaluation, or over the longer term either in "vestibule" evaluation at the job site or in the context of workshop performance.

An increasing number of school districts have acquired commercially available job performance sampling systems. Among these is the Singer System, an audiovisual system with a number of dedicated work stations including basic tools, bench assembly, drafting, electrical wiring, plumbing and pipefitting, carpentry and woodworking, refrigeration-heating-air conditioning, soldering and welding, office and sales clerk, needle trades, sheet metal, masonry, cooking and baking, small engine service, medical service, cosmetology, and data calculation and recording.

The JEVS System (Jewish Employment and Vocational Service), which measures potential in general industrial categories, includes twenty-eight work samples for hands-on assessment of skills, behaviors, and interests. Developed over a twenty-year period, and with normative data based on a national sample of over 1,100 students, the JEVS system has been used in a great many rehabilitation facilities. A maximum of five "clients" can be evaluated simultaneously by one evaluator. The work samples are organized in a hierarchy of increasing complexity, and results are directly related to ten worker-trait groups in the *Dictionary of Occupational Titles* (*DOT*). Included in the work samples are such areas as assembly/disassembly, binding, clerical, display and printing, electrical, industrial housekeeping, layout design and drafting, mail handling, mechanical, sorting, structural development, textile and tailoring, and metal work.

The TOWER evaluation system (developed over 10 years ago

by the ICD Rehabilitation and Research Center, NYC) involves work samples in jewelry manufacturing, leathergoods, clerical, drafting, drawing, welding, mail clerk, sewing, and electronics assembly. In the process of gathering these assessments, the student's work habits, work tolerance, work attitudes, work speed, and general motivation are also evaluated. In 1976, following extended research, a new *group*-oriented evaluation, called MicroTower, was introduced, offering a shorter period for evaluation.

The Valpar Component Work Sample Series consists of sixteen individual assessment units that have been normed on nonhandicapped workers, on special disability groups, and in terms of methods-time-measurement. The sixteen areas are small tools (mechanical), size discrimination, numerical sorting, upper body range of motion, clerical comprehension and aptitude, independent problem solving, multilevel sorting, simulated assembly, whole body range of motion, trilevel measurement, eye-hand-foot coordination, soldering and inspection (electronic), money handling, integrated peer performance, electrical circuitry and print reading, and drafting.

For purposes of illustration, we will describe and contrast two of the Valpar work samples, one that is dependent on eye-hand-foot coordination (#11) and one that involves teamwork with other workers (#14).

#11 (Eye-hand-foot coordination) (see Fig. 7)

PURPOSE: Measures eye-hand-foot coordination while simultaneously providing evidence of individual concentration, learning, planning, spatial discrimination, and reaction to immediate positive or negative feedback.

TASK: The individual sits at a tiltable box, with the forward/backward tilt being foot controlled and the side-to-side tilt being controlled by hand. The interior of the box is similar to a maze in which the task is to roll a series of balls along the channels without allowing them to drop in the holes along the way. The further the ball goes before landing in a hole the higher the points earned. Similarly, the more rapidly this is accomplished the better the time score will be.

DOT RELATIONSHIP: Involves skills that would be applicable

to laundry laborer, shoe repairman, heavy-equipment operator, injection molding machine operator, milling machine operator, drill press operator, punch press operator, offset press operator, mender, sewing machine operator, sheet metal worker, tow truck driver, fork lift operator, conveyor line operator.

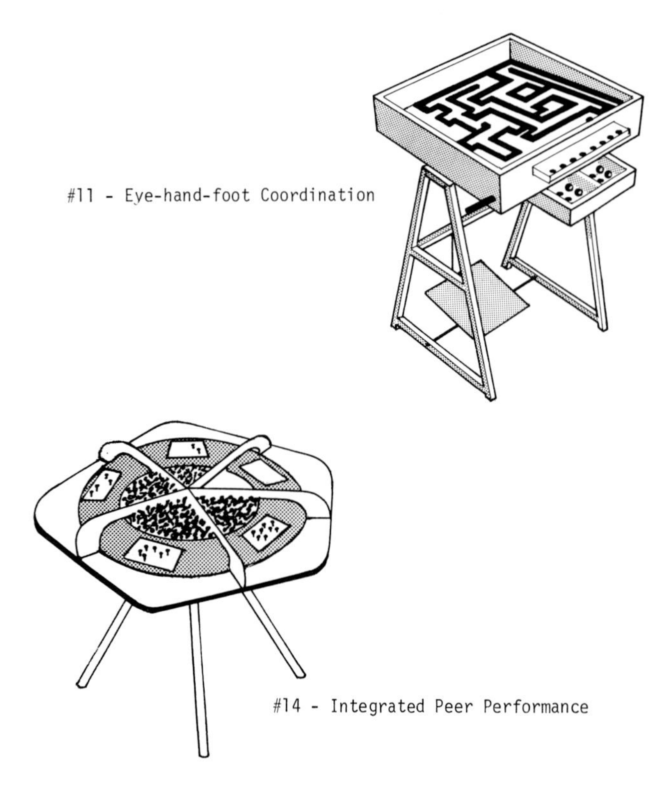

Figure 7. Two of the Valpar work samples.

#14 (Integrated Peer Performance)

PURPOSE: Measures assembly skills while simultaneously (and primarily) providing a measure of the human interaction that is involved in assembly line situations.

TASK: Five individuals sit around a small table on which a lazy Susan turntable is mounted. One station is occupied by the evaluator, who keeps time between task segments, scores the work done by each person on the task just completed, and monitors the ongoing work. The general nature of the task is to insert banana plugs into small assembly boards according to a color-coded set of instructions in pattern form. Each person is given the same amount of time inasmuch as the table rotates at fixed intervals, with the object being to assemble your plugs in the proper spaces. However, the stations are not of equal difficulty, and the set of tasks tends to be easier for the last assembler since the available holes are substantially reduced. This is counterbalanced by the frustrations encountered when a prior worker misplaces a plug in an incorrect hole. Norms are based on time elapsed and errors. Behavioral observations are especially important.

DOT Relationship: Involves skills that relate to manipulating, feeding-offbearing, handling, art work, sorting-inspecting-measuring, artistic restoration-decoration, miscellaneous customer service, accommodating work, ushering-messenger service, motion picture projection and photographic machinery work, news reporting, switchboard service, precision working, cropping-animal farming-gardening.

In setting up the Valpar evaluations, the instructor/evaluator is given explicit instructions to follow, thus ensuring a fair administration of the exercise across all persons being evaluated. Given below is an excerpt from the #11 job sample.

> Say: You will notice that on the bottom of the metal frame there is a foot pedal. This pedal is connected to the maze in the Work Box by a metal rod. When you move the pedal forward, the maze also moves forward. When you move the foot pedal back, the maze returns to its original position.
>
> NOTE: The client can use his right or left foot to operate the Foot Pedal. The evaluator should ask the client which foot he/she prefers to use.
>
> Say: Now, put your right (left) foot on the pedal and move the foot pedal and maze forward and backward until

you get a good feel for how they work together.

NOTE: The evaluator should allow the client to move the maze forward and backward four or five times or until the client gets a good idea of how the maze and foot pedal work together.

The Comprehensive Occupational Assessment and Training System (COATS) is commercially available from PREP, Inc., Trenton, NJ. As the name implies, this is a comprehensive vocational guidance package, aimed primarily at the nonhandicapped, but with potential usefulness for the mildly handicapped. The system has four major parts, which yield assessments of individual strengths and weaknesses in (1) work samples, (2) employability attitudes, (3) living skills, and (4) job matching. An important aspect of the COATS system is its use of computerized scoring and analysis of the individual's performance on the various test components. The work sample assessment is achieved through the use of audiovisual carrels with the occupational job sample materials being stored in small suitcases, allowing a carrel to be used in a multipurpose manner. Ten occupational areas are represented, including drafting, clerical-office, metal construction, sales, food preparation, medical services, travel services, barbering-cosmetology, and small engine. The living skills area of assessment is centered on adult basic competencies involving reading, writing, speaking-listening, computation, and problem solving in the knowledge areas of government-law, occupational knowledge, health, community resources, and consumer economics. While the COATS system is complex, requires a considerable amount of time, and may be unusable by blind or deaf persons, it nevertheless represents a comprehensive model that could be adapted for effective local use.

In spite of their potential, commercial systems are not inexpensive and may not always be suited to the handicapped person being tested, several having obvious drawbacks for persons with sensory impairments. Moreover, the selection of assessments may not accurately reflect local job market emphasis. For these reasons, a number of school districts have developed their own job samples and make them available for shared use at a location where evaluation can be accomplished in a scheduled class. The Long Beach (CA) School District, for example, has implemented such an approach. There, work sampling task assignments are used flexibly, depending on whether the student is mentally, orthopedically, visually, or otherwise handicapped.

It has been stated that a variety of work samples or job simulations is desirable for pre-vocational assessment. How extensive this sampling should be is, of course, arguable, but it is safe to say that to the extent that time and resources permit there should be more than one assessment in each of the occupational clusters for which curriculum offerings exist at the school. The development of a variety of job samples, especially those using local resources, should be undertaken in a deliberate way. Care should be taken to ensure that each job sample added to the collection is *not* redundant but instead adds to the fund of information about the student.

Suppose that a student was able to perform well in a work sample involving the task of assembly of nuts, bolts, and washers. Taken alone, that is about all that could be stated with assurance. However, by having the student do a variety of assembly tasks, such as union assembly, belt assembly, grommet assembly, telephone assembly, and lock assembly, a more reliable judgment can be made about his or her aptitudes in the *DOT* "Crafts/Manipulating" cluster. Moreover, this variation in tasks makes it possible to establish the level of complexity that the student can handle in task assignments, his or her frustration tolerance, and other worker traits that could bear on an occupational choice.

As an example, under the *DOT* classification of "Crafts/Manipulating," worker requirements involve a combination of (a) eye-hand coordination, (b) manual and finger dexterity, (c) spatial and form perception, (d) a decided preference for working with the hands, (e) the ability to work within prescribed standards and specifications, and (f) facility in adapting to a routine. In contrast, the *DOT* "Business/Accounting" classification shows worker requirements that include (a) ability to concentrate for long periods, (b) good vocabulary and verbal expression, (c) organizational ability, (d) speed and accuracy in making numerical determinations, (e) memory for detail, and (f) the ability to understand the principles of accounting, statistics, and fiscal management. Accordingly, work samples for students interested in these areas should reflect the variations in job requirements that are characteristic of jobs in those fields.

Using Behavioral Assessments

Work behaviors are critical to job survival, and they are also important contributors to being hired. Indeed, research (O'Neil, 1976) has established that the five most important qualities of an employee are

- being dependable
- giving an honest day's work
- knowing what is expected of you
- maintaining good health
- managing time and materials efficiently.

In the educational setting, estimations of an individual's eventual work adjustment can be arrived at through behavioral assessments. Quite simply, these are actions of the student that are seen or heard by an observer and that can be reliably counted.

Szoke and Vest (1975) have listed some twenty-six "behaviors" that are important both in educational and work contexts. They include the following:

1. ability to analyze and reason
2. attention span and work tolerance
3. cleaning up of work area
4. cooperation
5. dependability
6. enthusiasm
7. flexibility
8. grooming
9. initiation of own tasks
10. maturity in relation to group
11. neatness
12. perseverance
13. punctuality
14. reaction to frustration and stress
15. returning from breaks without being reminded
16. following safety instructions
17. seeking help when necessary
18. need for supervision
19. thoroughness
20. following verbal instructions
21. work attitude
22. work improvement with experience
23. work speed
24. following written instructions
25. emotional stability
26. self-confidence and self-concept

Though some of these (notably self-concept and self-confidence) are inferred rather than directly observed, all can be important elements of a behavior modification program in the event that this is called for by the instructional prescription for the handicapped student. Thus a learning disabled student, for example, may be involved in a behavior modification program aimed at increasing attention span and work tolerance, dependability, and punctuality, all very important to successful vocational training and eventual job success.

One community organization that serves young adult handicapped students (secondary level and above) has a multifaceted evaluation approach, involving various combinations of (a) personality tests, (b) interest tests, (c) achievement tests, (d) aptitude tests, (e) intelligence tests, (f) dexterity tests, (g) other tests, and (h) a variety of work sample systems. The following is a list of the evaluation options that exist at the Easter Seal Workshop in Burlingame, California.

List of Assessment Techniques Available for Use at the Evaluation Unit, Easter Seal Society for Crippled Children and Adults of San Mateo County (CA), Inc. (Reprinted by permission.)

Personality Tests

1. Gordon Personal Inventory — measures cautiousness, original thinking, personal relations, vigor.
2. Gordon Personal Profile — measures ascendancy, responsibility, emotional stability, sociability.
3. Survey of Personal Values — measures values that determine how an individual copes with everyday problems.
4. Survey of Interpersonal Values — measures critical values involving the individual's relationship with others.
5. California Life Goals — measures life goals defined as "future oriented" attitudes.
6. California Psychological Inventory — measures social interaction.
7. Work Environment Preference Schedule — assesses the

ability to work in a bureaucratic company.

8. Rotter's Incomplete Sentence Blank — allows the individual free expression.
9. Vocational Preference Inventory — yields a broad range of information about the individual.
10. 16 PF — assesses sixteen personality factors; test is available in Spanish and two reading levels.

Interest Tests

1. Kuder — indicates interest in ten broad areas.
2. Geist Picture Interest Inventory — is a nonverbal interest measure.
3. Picture Interest Inventory — is a nonverbal interest survey of six areas.
4. Gordon Occupational Checklist — is a non-academically oriented interest test.
5. WRIOT — is a nonverbal interest test.
6. Strong-Campbell Interest Inventory — includes general occupational themes and basic interests.

Achievement

1. Gates-MacGinitie Reading Test — a timed test of reading speed, accuracy, and vocabulary comprehension.
2. Personnel Tests for Industry — measures competence and verbal and numerical skills.
3. ABLE — measures vocabulary, reading, spelling, and math.
4. WRAT — measures spelling, math, and reading.
5. PIAT — a nonverbal achievement test measuring math, reading recognition, reading comprehension, spelling, general information.
6. Oral Directions — assesses general ability to follow directions recited from a cassette tape.
7. Adaptability — measures mental alertness or ability to follow directions.
8. College Qualification Test — three ability tests used by colleges in admission and placement.

Aptitude

1. General Clerical Test — measures aptitude for important clerical jobs.
2. Short Employment Test Battery — is a clerical aptitude test.
3. Flanagan Aptitude Classification Test — measures aptitude in thirty-one areas.
4. Bennett Mechanical Comprehension Test — measures the ability to perceive the relationship of physical forces and mechanical elements in practical situations.
5. Bennett Mechanical Comprehension Test, Spanish Edition — same as above.
6. Graves Design Judgment Test — measures certain components of aptitude for the appreciation and production of art structure.
7. Revised Minnesota Paper Form Board Test — is a nonverbal mechanical ability test requiring the capacity to visualize and manipulate objects in space.
8. Differential Aptitude Test — measures general scholastic aptitudes.
9. Appraisal of Occupational Aptitudes — measures clerical aptitude.

Intelligence

1. Revised Beta Exam — is a strictly timed, nonverbal measure of general mental ability.
2. Raven's Standard Progressive Matrices — is an untimed assessment of intellectual ability requiring abstract reasoning.
3. Army General Classification Test — is a verbal measure of general intelligence.
4. Slosson Intelligence Test — is an individual oral intelligence test.
5. *Western Personnel Test, Spanish Edition — is a five-minute general intelligence test.

Dexterity

1. Bennett Hand-Tool Dexterity Test — measures proficiency

in using mechanic's tools.
2. Minnesota Rate of Manipulation Test — measures gross movements of hands involving use of wrist.
3. Purdue Pegboard — measures finger dexterity.
4. Crawford's Small Parts Dexterity Test — measures fine eye-hand coordination.

Other Tests

1. Memory For Design Test — measures perceptual-motor coordination and is a sensitive indicator of brain damage.
2. Survey of Study Habits and Attitudes — in relation to academic pursuits.
3. Daily Living Skills — measuring skills necessary for daily functioning.
4. Blueprint Reading.
5. Cardpunch Operator — a shortly timed nonverbal test requiring cross-matching and quality control.

Work Sample Systems

1. WREST — is a horizontal test of achievement that can be used to confirm or reject diagnosis of mental retardation; consists of ten easy, homogeneous performances found in manual and clerical job situations in commerce, industry, and service: folding, stapling, packaging, measuring, assembling, tag stringing, pasting, collating, color and shade matching, and pattern matching.
2. Valpar — sixteen units measuring universal worker characteristics, keyed to the *Dictionary of Occupational Titles.*

    1. Small Tools
    2. Size Discrimination
    3. Numerical Sorting
    4. Upper Range of Motion
    5. Clerical
    6. Independent Problem Solving
    7. Multilevel Sorting
    8. Assembly
    9. Whole Body Range of Motion
    10. Trilevel Measurement
    11. Eye-Hand-Foot Coordination
    12. Soldering
    13. Money Handling
    14. Integrated Peer Performance
    15. Electrical Circuitry
    16. Drafting

3. JEVS — designed to reflect the primary skills inherent in

actual jobs. Twenty-eight units grouped into ten worker trait groups:

1. Handling — nut, bolt, and washer assembly; rubber stamping; washer threading; sign making.
2. Sorting, Inspecting, Measuring and Related Work — tile sorting; nut packing; collating leather samples.
3. Tending — grommet assembly.
4. Manipulating — union assembly; belt assembly; ladder assembly; metal square fabrication; hardware assembly; telephone assembly; lock assembly.
5. Routine Checking and Recording — filing by number; proofreading.
6. Classifying, Filing, Related Work — filing by three letters; nail and screw sorting; adding machine; payroll computation; computing postage.
7. Inspecting and Stock Checking — resistor reading.
8. Craftsmanship and Related Work — pipe assembly.
9. Costuming, Tailoring, and Dressmaking — blouse making; vest making.
10. Drafting and Related Work.

While numerous options may exist in an evaluation center such as the Easter Seal Workshop, it should be kept in mind that the choice of specific tests will vary from case to case. In one instance (Peter), a high school senior's summary profile included several assessments (See Fig. 8).

Noting that the results for this high school senior show below average eye-hand fine motor skills but superior performance in work samples where such skills are relevant, it is quite apparent that there may be contrasting results within a testing program for a given individual. Even more contradictory is the above average "conscientious" rating as indicated by the 16 PF personality test, coupled with the behavioral observations, which showed just the opposite during the testing. In such circumstances any "strength" shown in testing should be largely discounted since it is apparently not supported in practice. It is quite possible in Peter's case that emotional problems are the major concern and, on a day-to-day basis, could

Peter

TEST	RESULT
16 PF Personality test	— impatient, ambitious, conscientious
Strong-Campbell Interest Inventory	— domestic arts, office practice, law/politics, public speaking, merchandising
PIAT Achievement Test	— reading comprehension — grade 12.9, reading recognition — grade 10.6, mathematics — grade 8.4, spelling — grade 8.0
Slosson Intelligence and	— dull normal
Raven Progressive Matrices — (aptitude test omitted)	— average abstract reasoning
Crawford Small Parts Dexterity and	— below average in eye-hand fine motor coordination
Minnesota Rate of Manipulation Test	— very low in gross movements of hands/wrists
VALPAR	— Work Sample System — superior on small tools, size discrimination, numerical sorting, filing, independent problem solving, and soldering; above average on whole body range of motion; average on mail sorting and multilevel sorting; below average on assembly and eye-hand-foot coordination; very low on bookkeeping, tri-level measuring, money handling, integrated peer performance, and electrical circuitry.
Behavioral observations (as noted during the testing process)	— easily angered and suspicious, did not listen to instructions, impatient, easily distracted, slow-moving, easily confused, often late, appearance poor, left room without explanation, requested many breaks, and reported having physical pain (presumably after effects of an accident).

Figure 8. Summary of vocational evaluation.

markedly effect his performance. In this regard, it is well to keep in mind that testing *suggests but does not guarantee* how the student will actually perform in vocational training and, later, on the job.

In review, the IEP provided a starting point for the planning of the educational programming that is deemed most appropriate for the handicapped student. Vocational evaluation adds significantly to that body of information and gives an increased understanding of the student's vocational potential through structured assessment of his or her interests and occupational awareness, skills and capabilities, as well as work habits and interpersonal relationships that can bear on job performance.

Emphasis has been placed on the dual functioning of the special education and vocational education staff in the assessment process. In summary, this section has attempted to point out how the team concept can result in a comprehensive learner analysis profile. The highlights of this shared responsibility are shown below.

GOAL	SPECIAL EDUCATOR FUNCTION	VOCATIONAL EDUCATOR FUNCTION
Develop learner analysis profile	Evaluate quantitative numerical skills	Evaluate hobbies and other pertinent outside experiences or exposure
	Evalute verbal skills	
	Evaluate cognitive skills	Evaluate career awareness
	Evaluate perceptual skills	Evaluate vocational interests and aptitudes
	Evaluate language skills	Evaluate physical/manipulative skills
	Evaluate social skills	Evaluate work readiness
	Evaluate attitudes held	Evaluate work habits
	Evaluate personality factors	Participate in IEP steps, as requested
	Establish parental viewpoints	
	Participate in IEP steps	

CHAPTER 6

PLANNING OF APPROPRIATE CURRICULA AND THE IMPLEMENTATION OF INSTRUCTION

IN the previous section, considerable attention was given to the needs analysis for an individual student. That is, the student's unique makeup was the subject of evaluative activities by the special education staff and also by the vocational education staff. This section will focus on the prescription of an appropriate program of studies that is responsive to the identified needs. In these activities the vocational education staff will normally take the lead, though their effectiveness will very much be dependent upon the special education staff in a resource capacity.

Historically, vocational educators have had training and experience in the fields in which they are teaching and, therefore, are familiar with what skills and job requirements are normally expected at the entry level. Also, because of the way in which vocational education has been organized in the schools, the use of advisory committees made up of businessmen in the community helps to maintain a current awareness of those occupations reflected in the advisory committee membership. Curriculum design, then, generally reflects existing standards in an occupational field, with some accommodation to local trends and priorities. Such an approach lends itself quite well to the structuring of a generalized program for nonhandicapped students, but not nearly so well for the handicapped student whose program of studies must be individualized. For increased specificity in planning to be made feasible, it is essential that a more careful, finer grained study of the job be undertaken.

PLANNING AN APPROPRIATE CURRICULUM

Just as it is unfair to a student to provide training in a

subject matter that has no practical bearing on later life, it is unfair to provide vocational training for young people who would then be unable to find employment in that field. Accordingly, on a periodic basis, the staff in vocational education should make a survey of the job market to identify changing needs and trends that should be reflected in the school's vocational course offerings. As examples, consider the emergence of high technology (microminiaturized circuits, cryogenics, lasers, etc.) as a vocational area of increasing importance in a number of locations. In contrast, a more stable community in a rural area might find a continuing need for mechanics, agricultural workers, etc., but might find that the amount of job opportunities is apt to vary on a year-to-year basis. What is needed, then, is a systematic procedure for identifying changes in the job market, for analyzing the nature of the jobs that are available, for specifying the particular job requirements of the employers in terms that have significance to the instruction of a handicapped person, and for matching different individuals' strengths and weaknesses to these varying job requirements.

Figure 9 shows these steps in a simplified sequence and makes clear how the overall process leads to appropriate, individualized course design, while reflecting local job opportunities and broader vocational trends that are developing in society as a whole. This latter point is especially important considering that career advancement in this mobile society often means changing jobs *and* communities.

As can be seen in Figure 9, the first activity involves making a survey of the job market in the community. For purposes of illustration, we will assume that the school is interested in offering a course in horticulture, so the range of businesses that might be contacted could easily include a wholesale shrubbery nursery, retail plant nurseries, garden care firms serving light industry and suburban homes, florist shops, commercial flower greenhouses, a local golf course, the city park staff, and even the school district administrative offices. In the example shown in Figure 9, three of the businesses (the city park, the commercial greenhouses, and the retail nurseries) anticipated a future need for employees at an entry level and were further interested in providing a trial work situation for handicapped students

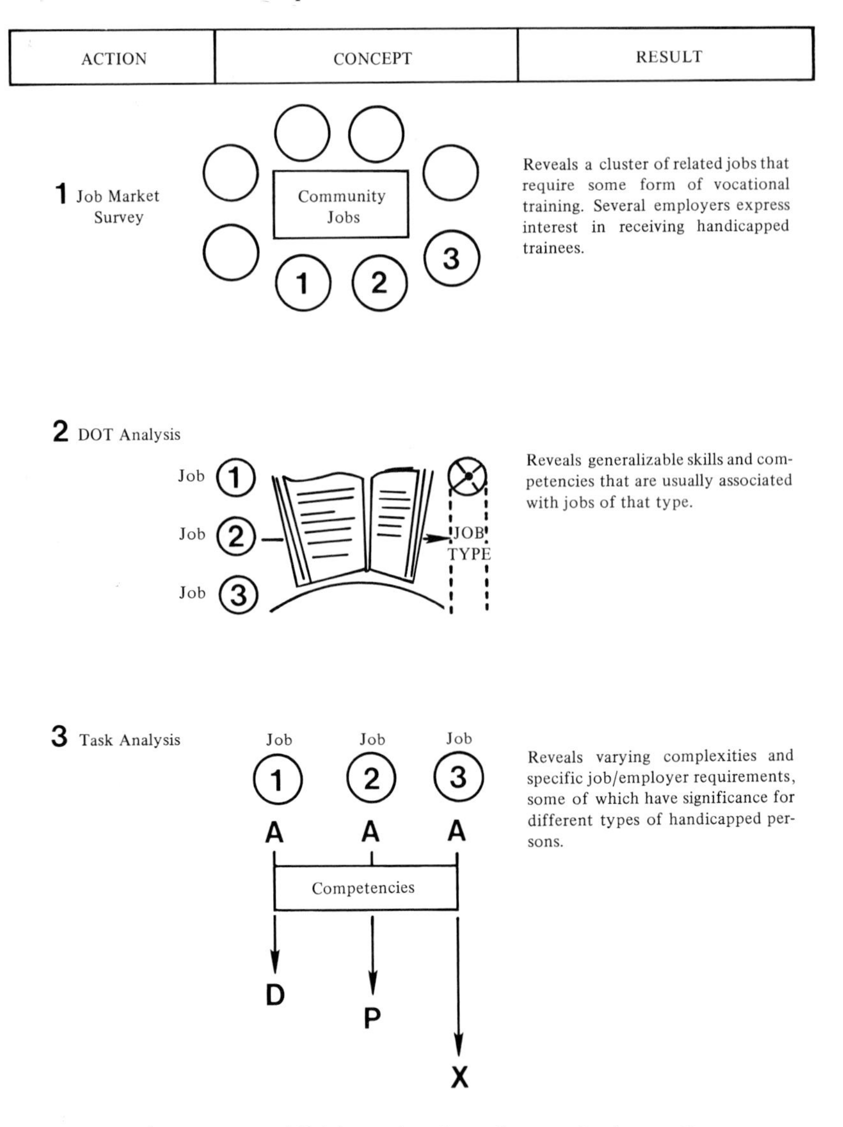

Figure 9. Establishing what is to be taught (page 1).

who might come through the training program.

The next activity would entail an examination of the *Dictionary of Occupational Titles* to determine the generalizable skills that are typically associated with jobs of these types in any community. Closely associated with the determination of

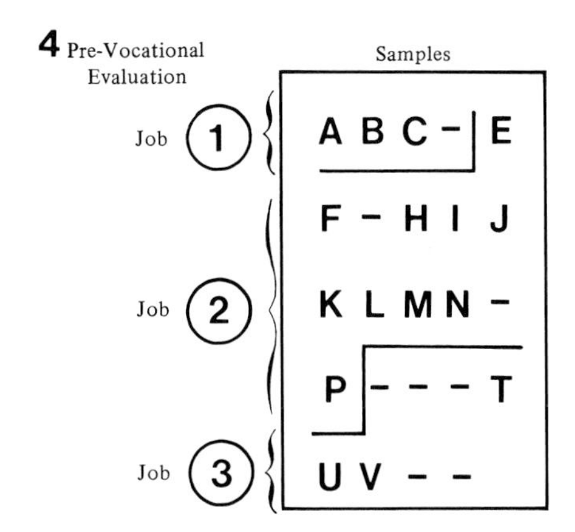

Assessment of an individual handicapped student reveals high potential for jobs 1 and 2, although there are special training needs in D, G, and O competencies; job 3 does not appear to be feasible at an entry level.

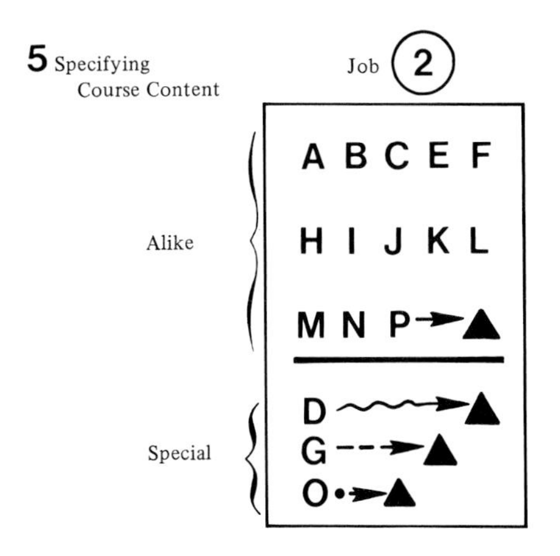

In organizing instruction for job #2, a better paying and more desirable job, most of the competencies could be taught to the desired competency level in a concurrent, similar manner for the handicapped and nonhandicapped. Three of the competencies will need specially planned course work or special resource assistance as indicated by the nature of the disability.

Figure 9. Establishing what is to be taught (page 2).

transferable skills is the need to establish the specific job requirements for each of the local employers. Naturally, these can be expected to vary in complexity and place different demands on the individual in terms of intellectual, social, perceptual, manipulative, and other skills. Further, they may differ in the extent to which rate of performance, allowable error rate, and amount of supervision effect the employability of different types of handicapped persons.

The third activity, then, consists of an on-site task analysis at the three businesses to establish exactly what is entailed in each job. In our horticulture example in Figure 9, the first job is the simplest, requiring competencies A through D. (In actual practice, of course, the number of competencies would be considerably greater, but in this illustration we are more concerned with relative complexity in the different jobs being analyzed.) Job #2 is more complex and requires that the entry level employee have competencies A through D *plus* E through P. Job #3 is still more complex and requires competencies A through X at a minimum. To carry through our example suppose that the first job was in the city park and consisted mainly of carrying out routine activities such as grass cutting, trimming, and fertilizing, plus the ability to follow directions from an on-site supervisor. Job #2 was in the commercial greenhouse, with added job requirements in the areas of repotting, flat preparation, etc. with more independence and responsibility for certain on-going tasks in the job. Job #3, in the retail nursery area, added further job complexity with a requirement for skills in dealing with customers. This could include a greater level of knowledge about the terminology and care of a wider variety of plants, the ability to make change, and the need to assist in the taking of inventories, just a few of the additional competencies required.

In the fourth activity in Figure 9, it can be seen that prevocational evaluation activities (using job samples in the horticulture field or in skills areas that are similar to it) have been carried out for one or more handicapped students. In the scoring of the individual's performance in the diagram, it is evident that aptitudes for D,G,O,Q,R,S,W, and X were lacking. Accordingly, the student appears to have the best job potential for the parks or the commercial greenhouse jobs, even though there are special training needs in competencies D, G, and O. Assuming that the commercial greenhouse job with greater complexity also pays better and has a better prospect for career advancement, it would appear that the handicapped student's individualized program of studies might well be tailored toward the commercial greenhouse job.

In activity #5 in Figure 9, the focus of attention is placed on the specification of course content that will help to prepare the handicapped student for a smooth transition from the training location to the work site. Because they are already identified as being important to the job, competencies A,B,C,E,F, H,I,J,K,L,M,N, and P should be taught. Because the handicapped student was able to demonstrate (through the work sample assessments) that he or she had aptitudes in those areas, it is possible that they could be taught in a similar manner to the nonhandicapped students, allowing, of course, for any adaptive techniques that might be required as a function of the disabling condition itself. Competencies D, G, and O, however, will probably need to be incorporated into the instructional program in a way that is unique to the needs of the handicapped individual and may not be taught the same way to the nonhandicapped. Were D related to the ability to follow directions, G related to the ability to count accurately, and O related to eye-hand coordination requirements, these should be taken into account at the time the handicapped student's course work is being planned.

It is important to establish that some competencies can be developed best by the vocational educator, some best by the special educator, and others may be only developed to a limited extent, with the result that job reengineering may have to be considered. For example, competency D could be assisted by the vocational educator through adaptations in his or her own teaching methods, giving shorter, more explicit assignments. Competency G might be best attacked by working collaboratively with the special educator to assist the student with basic math problems, using similar kinds of tasks (counting cuttings in making up a sixty plant flat would have easy parallels in the school resource room, using pencils, golf tees, or other substitutes). Competency O, depending on the nature of the eye-hand coordination required and the type of handicapping condition, might be satisfactorily resolved at the work site itself. Perhaps the particular task could be reassigned to another worker if it simply could not be performed. Perhaps some adaptive aid or device could be fabricated to provide the handicapped person with an easier task, or perhaps the employer would be willing to modify the way the job is done or the rate at which it is performed. In each case, then, the best strategy for providing the necessary instruction and/or assistance is sought for the particular handicapped student. Sometimes the solution will be apparent within the vocational education context, sometimes within the special education context, and sometimes only on the job itself.

It cannot be overstated that the planning process should be undertaken in a team fashion, with the special educator taking the initiative in blending the vocational course requirements with other academic studies, helping the vocational educator to determine appropriate signs of progress and points at which the program planning should be reevaluated, and suggesting strategies for instruction that will address specific areas of need. The vocational educator should take the initiative in determining the match between the task analysis and the individual's vocational evaluation with tests and work samples, then make changes in the course content to reflect job market factors and the potential of the individual, and revise his or her own instructional style as necessary. Also, and not to be overlooked, the student for whom individualized instruction is being planned should have input to the design process. While this is certainly limited in terms of the subject matter selection (the student presumably having little familiarity to bring to bear on these types of decisions) it is both fair and reasonable to involve the student in the goal-setting aspects of course planning and in the setting of the criteria by which adequate (or outstanding) performance will be judged.

In the more detailed discussions that follow, it is recognized that the procedures being recommended may be unfamiliar to the special education and vocational education staff. In such cases, information and assistance may be available from the local district office of the Department of Rehabilitation. Thus, the involvement of a rehabilitation counselor is viewed as an extension of the instructional planning team, capitalizing on the experience and knowledge of job opportunities for the handicapped that such persons typically possess.

JOB AND TASK ANALYSIS

As an early step toward the planning of relevant instruction, it has been recommended that attention be given to the nature of the job and the tasks required. To a large extent, vocational courses are designed to reflect general activities that are frequently encountered in an occupational cluster.

The use of a cluster identification form has been suggested by Phelps (1976) to delineate different course titles and/or major instructional units within an occupational area. Figure 10 shows Phelp's example of the breakdown for the ornamental horticulture occupational area. It can readily be seen that this method of display shows both the entry level jobs and possible career ladders.

Check: __ Exploration Cluster
_X_ Preparation Cluster

Cluster-Related Instructional Areas (course titles and/or major instructional units)	CAREER CLUSTER: *Ornamental Horticulture Occupations*			
Landscaping	*Groundskeeper*		*Landscape Gardener* *Landscape Designer*	*Landscape Architect*
Floriculture		*Flower Grower*	*Floral Designer*	*Florist*
Aboriculture	*Tree-Surgeon Helper*		*Tree-Trimming Foreman* *Tree Surgeon*	*Arborist*
Turf Management	*Greensworker*	*Greenskeeper* *Irrigation Controller*	*Superintendent, Greens* *Sod Grower* *Turf Supplies Salesman*	*Agronomist*
Nursery	*Laborer, Nursery* *Moss Handler* *Bagger-and-Burlap Man*	*Salesperson*	*Salesperson*	*Garden Center Manager* *Nursery Superintendent*
Greenhouse	*Greenhouse worker*		*Salesperson*	*Greenhouse Operator/ Manager*
LEVEL:	Laborer Loader Assistant Attendant Helper Tender Worker Sorter/ Packer	Operator Clerk Driver Installer Assembler Aide	Craftsman Supervisor Technician Inspector Complex Operator	Middle Manager Foreman Official

Figure 10. Cluster identification form.

The *Dictionary of Occupational Titles* is a good source of information about general activities associated with a particular occupational area or areas. Excerpts from the *DOT* in the "Horticultural Specialty Occupations" are shown below. It can be seen that many of the activities in the various occupational areas are closely aligned, but it is by no means certain that all the activities will be required of an individual who takes an entry level job in these related areas.

DOT Excerpts

405 HORTICULTURAL SPECIALTY OCCUPATIONS

This group includes occupations concerned with propagating and raising products, such as nursery stock, flowers, flowering plants, flower seeds, bulbs, and turf grasses. Also included are occupations concerned with growing food crops, such as mushrooms and rhubarb, which require controlled environmental conditions. Occupations concerned with propagating, raising, and transplanting forest trees are classified in Group 451.

405.684-014 HORTICULTURAL WORKER (agric.) I

Plants, cultivates, and harvests horticultural specialties, such as flowers and shrubs, and performs related duties in environmentally-controlled structure applying knowledge of environmental systems: Ascertains growing schedules and deviations from established procedures from grower or manager. Sows seed and plants cuttings. Looks at and feels leaf texture, bloom development, and soil condition to determine nutrient and moisture requirements and to detect and identify germ and pest infestations. Sets fertilizer timing and metering devices that control frequency and amount of nutrients to be introduced into irrigation system. Applies herbicides, fungicides, and pesticides to destroy undesirable growth and pests, using spray wand connected to solution tank. Reads and interprets sensing indicators and regulates humidity, ventilation, and carbon dioxide systems to control environmental conditions. Grafts scions to seedling stock. Pollinates, prunes, transplants, and pinches plants, and culls flowers, branches, fruit, and plants to insure development of marketable products. Harvests, packs, and stores crop, using techniques appropriate for individual horticultural specialty. May maintain and repair hydroponic and environmental control systems. May maintain and repair structures, using materials, such as corrugated fiberglass panels, lath, glass panes, and putty, and tools, such as hammer, saw, and putty knife. May be designated according to work location as GREENHOUSE WORKER (agric.); according to techniques employed as HYDROPONICS WORKER (agric.); or according to horticultural specialty as ORCHID WORKER (agric.).

405.687-010 FLOWER PICKER (agric.)

Harvests flowers, such as daffodils and tulips, working as

member of crew; Pinches or cuts flower stem to remove flower from plant. Bundles specified number of stems, using rubberband, and carries bundles to collection box.

406 GARDENING AND GROUNDSKEEPING OCCUPATIONS

This group includes occupations concerned with caring for areas, such as gardens, grounds, parks, and cemeteries. Landscaping occupations are classified in Group 408.

406.683-010 GREENSKEEPER (any ind.) II laborer, golf course.

Performs any combination of the following duties, as directed by GREENSKEEPER (any ind.) I, to maintain grounds and turf of golf course in playing condition: Operates tractor, using specific attachments, to till, cultivate, and grade new turf areas, to apply prescribed amounts of lime, fertilizer, insecticide, and fungicide, and to mow rough and fairway areas at designated cut, exercising care not to injure turf or shrubs. Cuts turf on green and tee areas, using hand mower and power mower. Connects hose and sprinkler systems at designated points on course to irrigate turf. Digs and rakes ground to prepare new greens, grades and cleans traps, and repairs roadbeds, using shovels, rakes, spades, and other tools. May plant, trim, and spray trees and shrubs.

406.684-014 GROUNDSKEEPER, INDUSTRIAL-COMMERCIAL (any ind.) caretaker, grounds; gardener; yard laborer.

Maintains grounds of industrial, commercial, or public property, performing combination of following tasks: Cuts lawns, using hand mower or power mower. Trims and edges around walks, flower beds, and walls, using clippers and edging tools. Prunes shrubs and trees to shape and improve growth, using shears. Sprays lawn, shrubs, and trees with fertilizer or insecticide. Rakes and burns leaves and cleans or sweeps up litter, using spiked stick or broom. Shovels snow from walks and driveways. Spreads salt on public passage ways. Plants grass, flowers, trees, and shrubs. Waters lawn and shrubs during dry periods, using hose or by activating fixed or portable sprinkler system. Repairs fences, gates, walls, and walks, using carpentry and masonry tools. Paints fences and outbuildings. Cleans out drainage ditches and culverts, using shovel and rake. Depending on size and nature of employing establishment, uses tractor equipped with attachments, such as mowers, lime- or fertilizer-spreaders, and lawn roller. May perform variety of laboring duties, common to type of employing establishment, when yard work is completed.

406.687-010 GROUNDSKEEPER, PARKS AND GROUNDS (gov. ser.) park worker.

Keeps grounds of city, State, or national park and playgrounds clean and repairs buildings and equipment: Mows lawns, using hand mower or power-driven lawnmower. Grubs and weeds around bushes, trees and flower beds and trims hedges. Picks up and burns or carts away paper and rubbish. Repairs and paints benches, tables, guardrails, and assists in repair of roads, walks, buildings, and mechanical equipment, using handtools. Cleans comfort stations and other buildings. May live on site and be designated CAMPGROUND CARETAKER (gov. ser.).

Task analysis calls for a more detailed look at the job to determine those particular requirements which might affect the potential job performance of different handicapped students. Moyer and Dardig (1978) have pointed out several ways in which special educators can become involved in task analysis, hopefully by working together with vocational educators. Three of the more common alternatives are as follows:

1. *Observing* a person who is already proficient in the task. This is an efficient procedure, but because of the proficiency of the performer, tasks may be accomplished very quickly, masking key elements that are important to beginners.
2. *Trying* a task oneself, noting each step that is necessary as it is being performed. This procedure is likely to take too long since it presumes a certain amount of learning by the task analyzer.
3. *Backwards chaining* from the terminal objective, specifying the pyramid of tasks leading to successful accomplishment of the overall goal. This procedure relies heavily on a logical analysis process, and needs to be verified for its accuracy by persons who are fully familiar with

the tasks involved.

Brolin (1976) has suggested that analysis of job requirements should focus on (1) computation skills, (2) measurement skills, (3) communication skills, (4) physical demands, (5) working conditions, (6) manipulative activities, (7) special conditions, e.g. distractions, training, responsibility, and (8) personal qualifications, e.g. reliability, appearance, safety.

Figure 11 suggests one way for organizing a task analysis form for use in on-site job description. Note that the upper part of the form can be partially completed ahead of time on the basis of *DOT* descriptions and advance knowledge about the job.

A critical feature of task analysis for the handicapped is not only the observation of customary processes within the job, but the context in which these processes are performed. It is important to know, for example, the extent to which the work setting is adaptable to use by persons in wheelchairs (aisles of greenhouses would not normally be accessible, and the humidity and reaching involved would tend to make this job impractical). Similarly, it is important to establish the extent to which job re-engineering can be considered to bypass certain tasks that are clearly impossible, such as color differentiation by the blind.

ADAPTATION OF THE CURRICULUM AND THE TRAINING PROGRAM

It is extremely unlikely that any vocational education course will need to be totally redesigned to accommodate handicapped students. At the same time, it is quite likely that adjustments will have to be made on an individual basis for different handicapped students. These changes fall into several categories, including

- *Procedural changes*
  - — in instructor's presentational techniques
  - — in the schedule and sequence of instruction
  - — in the instructional materials
  - — in the way aides or student peers are used

BUSINESS FIRM: ________ CONTACT: ________ DATE: ________________

GENERAL INFORMATION

DOT OCCUPATIONAL AREA: __________ DOT CODE NUMBER: ________

SHORT DOT DESCRIPTION: ____

____

____

JOB TITLE AT BUSINESS FIRM: ____________________________________

PRETRAINING REQUIREMENTS: ______________________________________

PAY RATE (ENTRY): ______ CAREER OPPORTUNITIES: ________________

SPECIFIC INFORMATION

PRIMARY WORK SETTING: INDOOR ____ OUTDOOR ____ BOTH ______

ACCESS TO WORK STATION: ____

ACCESS TO SUPPLIES AND EQUIPMENT: ______________________________

LIGHTING: ____ HOT/COLD: ____ HUMID/DRY: ____ VENTILATION: ____

HAZARDS: ________________ TRAVEL NEEDS: ________________________

INTERPERSONAL RELATIONSHIPS:

INFREQUENT __________ MODERATE __________ OFTEN __________

AMOUNT OF SUPERVISOR CONTACT: ____ CUSTOMER CONTACT: ____

AMOUNT OF TEAMWORK WITH OTHER EMPLOYEES: ________________

OBSERVED MAJOR TASK SEQUENCES: _________________________________

____

____

____

____

____

____

Figure 11. Guidesheet for on-site task analysis (page 1).

PRINCIPAL ELEMENTS OF THE TASK PERFORMANCE:

VERBAL FACILITY AND COMMUNICATION ____ DEXTERITY ________

COMPUTATIONAL AND NUMERICAL ________ COORDINATION ______

KNOWLEDGE AND MEMORY ________ STRENGTH ________

VISUAL DIFFERENTIATION ________ BENDING ________

AUDITORY DIFFERENTIATION ________ LIFTING ________

GRASPING AND TURNING ________ REACHING ________

OTHER ________

PRINCIPAL PERFORMANCE REQUIREMENTS:

PIECE RATE OR EFFICIENCY ________ RELIABILITY ________

ERROR RATE OR PRECISION ________ PUNCTUALITY ________

PROBLEM SOLVING ________ CREATIVITY ________

INDEPENDENCE ________ TOLERANCE ________

OTHER ________

SPECIAL IMPLICATIONS FOR HANDICAPPED PERSONS:

BARRIERS TO BE REMOVED OR MODIFIED: ________

____

SPECIAL EQUIPMENT NEEDS: ________

____

SPECIAL TRAINING NEEDS: ________

____

OTHER: ________

____

Figure 11. Guidesheet for on-site task analysis (page 2).

- *Facilities changes*
  - — in the equipment used
  - — in the physical work station
  - — in access to the classroom and its contents
- *Performance changes*
  - — in the objectives to be achieved

— in the methods by which tasks may be accomplished
— in rate or accuracy requirements (modifications of work standards)

The vocational educator should be aware that modifications in the instructor's presentational techniques (and other types of changes as well) are made on a case-by-case basis. If the handicapped student is mildly retarded it is very likely that changes in the instructor's presentational style would include

- more repetition of key points;
- breaking down instruction into small steps;
- providing simple job aids;
- setting incremental, short-term goals;
- increasing the use of "see-do" demonstrations.

If the student is learning disabled the instructor might modify his or her instruction by

- providing positive reinforcement for student achievements (even modest ones);
- emphasizing a supportive environment in the classroom;
- reflecting the student's preferred learning modality when making a choice of instructional techniques;
- checking closely on student performance when tasks are dependent on perceptual, psychomotor, or other processing abilities;
- minimizing classroom distractions.

If the student is visually handicapped or blind, techniques might include

- modifying certain equipment by adding safety features, braille, or other special markings;
- orienting the student (hands-on) to supplies and equipment, and arranging consistent location of the student's own materials;
- providing instructional handouts early enough that they can be brailled in advance of class use;
- orally stating what is occurring in demonstrations.

If the student is deaf or hard of hearing, techniques might include

- maintaining eye contact with the student during any and all oral presentations to facilitate speech reading;
- temporary use of an interpreter;
- using visual aids (including captioned materials) to illustrate key points;
- providing special practice in technical vocabulary;
- listening attentively and encouraging oral communication by the student.

If the student is orthopedically handicapped, techniques might include

- assuring that the student can see all instructional demonstrations;
- providing assistance (teacher or peer) for any physical task beyond the student's capabilities;
- providing assistive devices (jigs, etc.) to facilitate physical tasks;
- assuring that the student can reach and manipulate necessary equipment.

The preceding examples are necessarily rather general in nature and are not meant to be exhaustive of the various ways in which a vocational instructor might modify the instructional process to better serve a particular handicapped student. The nature and extent of the handicap, together with the results of individual assessment of the student's initial capabilities, will be the chief determinants of the kinds and numbers of changes that should be made in the regular instructional program.

At a more specific level, when one or more of the above changes in instructional technique are being attempted, the special educator can be of great help to the vocational educator. Some examples will illustrate this point.

Example #1: John is severely visually handicapped, enrolled in a high school woodworking class, and faced with an assignment that involves (1) measuring a board to be cut, (2) handcutting the board at a true 90° angle, (3) countersinking a row of finishing nails spaced about one-half inch from the board edge, and (4) mounting hinges flush with the board edge.

In reviewing these tasks ahead of time, the vocational educator and the special educator decide to (1) have the student use a special ruler with raised markings to determine the proper length, (2) use a carpenter's square as a saw guide when starting the handsaw cut, (3) provide separate practice on another board before using the countersink punch on the final product, and (4) use a second board placed in a protruding manner over the edge of the board on which the hinges will be mounted, thus serving as a guide for flush alignment of the edge of the hinge with the edge of the board.

Example #2: Irene is deaf, newly enrolled in a dental assisting class at a regional occupational program, and faced with an assignment involving a class demonstration in which new vocabulary will be introduced.

In a planning meeting between the special educator and the vocational educator, the question is raised whether an interpreter is needed. Because the student is a good speechreader, they feel that this expense can be avoided simply by (1) providing an advance study vocabulary list, which the student should learn to speech-read as well as pronounce, (2) seating the student advantageously for the demonstration, (3) having the instructor face the student when speaking, then alternate the demonstrations and explanations, and (4) having a "buddy" in the class take duplicate notes with the use of a carbon sheet.

Example #3: Wally has a learning handicap in that he becomes hyperactive as a result of excessive envionmental stimulation. He has enrolled in typing class, but there is considerable doubt as to how he will respond in a room full of noisy typewriters.

In consultation, the special educator and vocational educator decide to (1) assign seating that will hold visual and noise distraction to a minimum, (2) monitor Wally's first few classes very closely to see whether any problems develop, (3) establish personal short-term goals with Wally, making sure that he realizes he is not in a competitive race with the rest of the class, and (4) provide "make up" sessions and tutorings if and when Wally falls behind.

Example #4: Mary is educable mentally retarded and is entering a work study program through which she hopes to get work in a large discount store. She is faced with the problem of adjustment to a regular work schedule, taking directions from a new supervisor, and "too many" new things to learn about the job.

The special educator and work study coordinator meet to discuss the work site situation and the major elements of concern that should be addressed. They agree that early success is very important and, therefore, decide that the employer should be asked to (1) start the student with a simple, highly repetitive task that can be reasonably closely monitored, (2) have an experienced, helpful employee demonstrate the task and "phase-in" the student in small steps, (3) acknowledge the development of new skills and appropriate work habits through immediate positive reinforcements, and (4) implement a deliberate program of rotation through various tasks in the store to find those which the student seems able to perform reliably.

Some Key Adjustments for Mainstreamed Handicapped Students

Each handicapped student will exhibit individual differences, including various work interests and capabilities and, therefore, may require different kinds of adjustments on the part of the instructional staff, modification of the facilities, or adaptation in the nature of the work task itself. Nevertheless, there are some fairly consistent and predictable issues that are likely to arise when any handicapped student is mainstreamed in with regular vocational students. Both the special educator and the vocational educator need to be sensitive to these issues and, to the extent possible, allow for them in their planning process.

The first issue involves integrating the handicapped student into the class routine. A critical aspect of this is the extent to which open, effective classroom communication is implemented between the instructor and the handicapped student and between the handicapped student and the nonhandicapped peers. The second issue involves a fair allocation of instructor time to the handicapped student and also to the other non-handicapped students. The third issue involves the setting of vocational goals and standards that are meaningful and equitable. The fourth issue involves the reasonableness of expenditures to facilitate the handicapped student's vocational education. The fifth involves the placement of handicapped students in appropriate work study and work experience settings with a view toward increasing their post-schooling independence and self-reliance.

While each of these topics is large and often complex in nature, some general strategies can be suggested.

INTEGRATION AND COMMUNICATION: Mainstreamed handicapped students seem to be well accepted by their nonhandicapped peers in the vast majority of schools. Often they become a natural part of the scene, with peers eventually tending to forget the students' apparent limitations, and the teacher forgetting to "teach-down," both sometimes leading to surprising results.

Where integration into the mainstream has been smoothest there usually has been an early emphasis on naturalness, easy acceptance, and a matter-of-factness in the teacher's approach. It is safe to assume that overt resistance to integration on the part of the host teacher will generate trouble, simply because the nonhandicapped students will pick up on this behavior and similarly resist the handicapped person without real justification.

This does not mean that all teachers should be expected to welcome handicapped students without reservation, for many of them have understandable doubts and insecurities about their own ability to give the student what he or she needs. While this is an understandable situation it also is not an adequate excuse, for the requisite skills and techniques can be learned while doing, can be acquired through in-service study, and can be enhanced through organized cooperation with the special education teacher.

When the handicapped student is made to feel that he or she

belongs in the class, then "little" things (like the willingness to ask questions in front of peers) will help to prevent communication breakdowns and lead to better mutual understanding. Thus, a hard-of-hearing student who feels comfortable enough to tell a teacher that only *part* of the lecture was understood, because the teacher had turned away while talking, will really be helping the teacher to do a better job in future lectures while at the same time avoiding the possible stigma of seeming to appear slow or inattentive.

Most handicapped students prefer to be involved in regular class activities, doing things the other students do. This is sometimes difficult when the student cannot keep up the pace, shows lack of comprehension, or otherwise needs help. Nevertheless, completely separating the student through special and different assignments is not advisable. Rather, the use of adaptive procedures to involve the student is much to be preferred.

If the student's handicap is not readily apparent, then the teacher's approach to involving the student in the classroom routine may be subtle, perhaps through a quietly established buddy system or merely through minor changes in classroom procedures. If the student's handicap is readily apparent, and especially if the physical aspects of the condition are "repugnant" or "antisocial," e.g. spasticity or drooling by the cerebral palsied, a *brief* discussion with the class about the student's problem and special needs will cut short much misunderstanding. Note that discussion should not be wholly negative but should also point up what the handicapped student *can* do independently. This brief session can occur before the student arrives in the class or, if the special educator states that the particular student has learned to deal with this kind of situation constructively, can directly involve the handicapped student in the discussion. Interesting examples of this candid discussion among young persons regarding their handicaps are shown in the "*Feeling Free*" television series produced by the American Institutes for Research and aired in 1978 by many public broadcasting stations across the country.

In effect, then, the minimum amount of disruption in classroom routine is the best course of action. A smooth, relaxed feeling about a more seriously handicapped student can often be achieved by being matter-of-fact and "upfront" about the student's needs and abilities. In any case, isolation from the regular students is most definitely to be avoided if it is ever anticipated that the handicapped student will enter the mainstream of society as a young adult.

FAIR ALLOCATION OF INSTRUCTOR TIME: Each time the statement is made that the handicapped student needs individualized, personally tailored instruction there is apt to be concern that this will have an impact on the instructor's time and will reduce the time available to other, nonhandicapped students. It is not possible to deny that extra time is often needed, but it is reasonable to assume that a suitable time allocation is possible so that other students' needs are not ignored.

One way that instructor time can be fairly shared by the handicapped and nonhandicapped class members is through strategic placement of the student in the room where the instructor can (a) lend assistance while demonstrating a process, (b) check frequently on the individual's progress while passing by, (c) involve other willing students who can help, and (d) assure easy access to needed supplies and equipment that the handicapped student might need.

Certainly, no regular instructor should expect to become completely tutorial in dealing with one handicapped student while simultaneously maintaining a group focus for instruction of the nonhandicapped. Through the use of such instructional techniques as short-term "study contracts," however, it is possible to accomplish a considerable amount of personalized instruction without impeding the progress of any student or groups of students. Since contracts are necessarily accomplished on an individual basis, it is clear that they provide a great deal of flexibility in allowing students to proceed at their optimal rate toward relevant, known goals. This can benefit the nonhandicapped as well as the handicapped.

In the last analysis, fair distribution of a teacher's time is *not* a case of the handicapped against the nonhandicapped. Rather, fairness should be defined as a distribution of the teacher's time in proportion to students' needs. With this definition in mind it is understandable and fair that mainstreamed handicapped students may indeed deserve and benefit from extra teacher time, though often this is not essential.

SETTING GOALS AND STANDARDS: In an earlier section the role of job/task analysis was discussed in terms of its importance to vocational curriculum planning. In that regard, the world of work, even in a rather narrowly defined occupational area, calls for a variety of skills and knowledge by persons holding similarly titled entry level jobs. Accordingly, the a priori standards and the list of performance skills that should be mastered in any given vocational course as set by state, local, or school curriculum committees are likely to be arbitrary, and in many instances would not match the necessary, i.e. employer required, skills a student needs to qualify for a particular job. Indeed, the skills that an employer seeks in a "new hire" will usually be defined by one or more of several factors, such as (1) whether the job consists of operating a particular machine, in which case the job is essentially defined by factors having to do with the design of the equipment, (2) whether the company work force is large or small, which will influence the degree of specificity versus generality in job responsibilities, and (3) whether there is a unique precedent for the job, perhaps established by a prior employee, which will affect the number of options open for redefining job elements.

In the light of the above, it is realistic to recognize that *in point of fact* each student in a vocational class does *not* need identical training leading toward identical goals and standards. It is much better to take the position that the vocational educator, together with the special educator, should *adjust* course goals and standards in the light of individual differences and job opportunities. That is, the potential of a particular student may be limited by a disability in such a way that some standards and goals cannot be met. This does not mean that such a student is a "failure" (and should receive a low course grade) but rather that those specific accomplishments that *were achieved* should be made known so that a prospective employer would be able to judge whether the individual could fill a particular job.

What is needed, then, is a shift away from normative

grading, yielding letter grades that have no intrinsic meaning, toward criterion-referenced grading, yielding brief statements of demonstrated competencies that would be meaningful to employers.

Maintaining a flexible stance with respect to the setting of course standards and individual goals is an important key to this kind of practical, work-oriented student evaluation. In perspective, this may be one of the most difficult general issues to address because of the traditions in education that have sustained normative grading and also because of long-standing assumptions by many vocational educators that they should not "certify" graduates of a course unless they have demonstrated skills to pre-set standards. This latter view ignores the fact that schools produce people, not identical products on an assembly line.

REASONABLENESS OF EXPENDITURES TO SERVE THE HANDICAPPED: Currently, when federal, state, and local government taxation is being questioned and the competition for limited tax dollars is acute, it is appropriate to examine the pros and cons of expenditures designed to meet the special needs of handicapped students. As is evidenced by the number of court cases arising out of recent legislation (particularly Section 504 regulations), in which disputes have developed over whether an institution had or had not provided sufficient access, resources, or assistance to handicapped students, there is no simple answer to what is reasonable in the way of expenditures.

No one would argue that every piece of equipment, every desk in a room, or every work station should be modified on the mere chance that a handicapped person (with some undefined disability or disabilities) may sometime use it. On the other hand, few would argue that limiting the handicapped person's performance by limiting access to necessary equipment, desks, or rooms is inconsistent with the law requiring nondiscriminatory practices.

Whether the issue is the modification of tangible facilities such as those just mentioned, the provision of support services such as transportation to a work site, the help of a specialist (interpreter, braillist, evaluator, etc.), or the reallocation of funds to carry out direct instruction (modified student-teacher ratios or the addition of teacher aides), it is clear that priorities will have to be set, and the principle of parsimony should govern decisions about expenditures.

Another way of looking at the problem, and one that is consistent with the overall goals of education, is to recognize that each handicapped individual, like nonhandicapped ones, seeks to be as independent and self-reliant as possible as an adult. The school's function is to help the student achieve this as efficiently as possible. In that vein, job survival skills, the ability to move from one job site to another, and the chance to move up a career ladder are all influenced positively by the individual's *natural* adaptability. They are negatively influenced by the amount of stipulations and pre-conditions that must be accommodated before the job can be performed.

To illustrate, consider the possibility that an orthopedically handicapped student (confined to a wheelchair) is interested in pursuing a distributive occupation. If the individual wants to work in an auto parts store, a library, or similar work setting, potential problems immediately arise associated with the shelving of items. Certainly, remodeling the autoparts store or the library is impractical. What are the alternatives and what might be a cost-effective approach?

Recognizing that each case will have to be addressed in terms of its own specifics, the following steps could be tried.

1. Initially, pending the individual's confirmation of the occupational choice through initial coursework and exploratory exposure to the kind of work involved, expenditures can be held to a minimum by incorporating in the training situation a "buddy system" (for reaching purposes) and by selecting a work situation where functional problems are minimized (wide aisles, low shelves).
2. To the extent that the individual's interests and aptitudes indicate that a career is possible in the occupational area but the potential for employment is limited by the access problem, it *may* be possible to acquire through the Department of Rehabilitation (under the Rehabilitation Services Administration) a new type of wheelchair that can be electrically narrowed by the operator until it fits through restricted

access aisles or doors. Similarly, it is possible to seek the assistance of the professional staff at one of a number of RSA's rehabilitation engineering centers across the country. These engineers are experts in the design and fabrication of special purpose equipment and might make a reaching/grasping appliance that the handicapped individual could use effectively from the wheelchair.

The preceding example is not so farfetched as it may sound. The case study that follows is an actual application of the latter approach, which has been reported in the literature on rehabilitation.

Case History

A triple amputee of both legs and the upper right arm was successfully employed as a clerk in a motorcycle parts store. He wore a prosthesis on the stump of his right arm. With it he could propel a regular wheelchair. But his left arm and hand had to do everything else. That put a heavy burden on the one arm. The client was also able to drive his automobile with hand controls.

There was only one major problem. At work he couldn't reach up to the top shelves to get spare parts for customers. All the parts were placed in cardboard boxes of similar size and strength. To solve his problem a reaching device had to be designed to meet the following specifications:

1. The device had to be lightweight.
2. It had to be operated by one hand, the left one.
3. It had to be able to hold a box of parts securely while the client lowered it to within his reach.
4. The device had to be well constructed as it would be used many times a day.

The solution was a spring-loaded clamp secured to the end of a lightweight pole. When the client pressed a control lever in his hand, the clamp opened and grasped the box. The client then permitted the device to slip through his hand, bringing the box down to within his reach.

This device was designed, constructed and tested on the job within a week and contributed to the continued employment of the client.

In brief, the key principles relating to barrier removal are

- expenditures relating to *basic* barrier removal (ramps, equipment access, transportation etc.), which will be shared by handicapped students now and in the future, are legitimate and necessary under the law;
- minor expenditures that can importantly add to an individual's *education and training* (braille micrometers, talking calculators, special materials, etc.) should be made available *on loan* to students who need them;
- significant expenditures directly affecting the *employability* of a person (acquiring tools and devices, unique fabrication of specific job aides, re-engineering of a work station, etc.) can often be accomplished through close coordination with the Department of Rehabilitation, local community agencies or service groups, or even *purchase* by the employer.

Finally, it should be pointed out that the true "reasonableness" of expenditures for a handicapped person should *not* rest on whether he or she "costs more" to educate than a nonhandicapped person, who clearly has less critical needs. Instead, it should be based on whether as a result of those expenditures the handicapped individual's chances of becoming a productive wage earner rather than a long-term welfare recipient are enhanced.

GAINING APPROPRIATE WORK EXPERIENCE: It is an unusual secondary student who is sure and confident about the occupation that he or she would like to pursue as an adult. A handicapped student is doubly uncertain, often because of limited exposure to the world of work.

When the community is centered around marine, forestry, or agricultural occupations, the likelihood of an obvious career choice increases, but still is by no means certain when individual differences are taken into account. In the three occupations mentioned, for example, many jobs involve physical strength and endurance, agility and mobility, and require an ability to work outdoors under varying climatic conditions and on sharply varied surfaces or terrains. Such conditions can be accommodated by a deaf student or a mentally retarded student, but they seriously limit the options open to an orthopedically handicapped or other health-impaired person, or a blind or visually handicapped person.

It is evident from this example that vocational training programs should maintain a balance between specialized course offerings that are appropriate to the local job market and course offerings that are exploratory, being primarily designed to give students exposure to jobs they might qualify for elsewhere. Fortunately, the handicapped, like the rest of our society, are becoming more mobile and willing to move to take advantage of promising job opportunities.

If one accepts the premise that vocational training is going to be most useful and relevant if it closely resembles the tasks inherent in the job itself, then it follows that training for particular elements of local jobs may also have applicability elsewhere, in jobs where the negative aspects are missing. Thus, small engine servicing has applicability to the marine, forestry, and agriculture occupations but also has relevance to appliance, motorcycle, lawnmower repair, and to other fields that do not involve sustained, heavy, outdoor work.

This exposure to various occupational areas should occur both in training settings and in work settings even where local business and industry are lacking. The latter is obviously more difficult to achieve if one thinks only in terms of work experience placement directly in the business community. By looking at the example of sheltered workshops, however, a lesson can be learned. In seeking contract work that can be done at the workshop, and which requires only minimal space and equipment, these organizations create job environments that broaden the work exposure and work opportunities for handicapped persons.

It is not unreasonable to assume, for instance, that a large business in a highly technological field will have fairly rapid turnover in its equipment to keep abreast of emerging technological developments or to achieve greater work productivity. Such a firm might willingly donate its out-of-date equipment and perhaps provide a limited amount of professional help to a school (not necessarily a local one) if the school offers a plan in which it proposes to set up a job simulation station. In the event that saleable products eventually could be produced at this job simulation station, it is within the realm of possibility that the supplying company would also be a potential purchaser.

In sum, resourcefulness and flexibility are important aspects of any vocational program that hopes to offer a wide range of occupational training and job-relevant experience in which handicapped students can participate. A reasonable balance should be maintained between training for local job opportunities and the provision of other options that handicapped (and other) students might want to pursue.

SETTING AND MONITORING GOALS AND OBJECTIVES

Goals exist at many levels for any given student. For the handicapped student in vocational education some examples are

- life goals — "to achieve independence and self-reliance"
  — "to be gainfully employed in a chosen occupation"
- school goals — "to complete the requirements for graduation on schedule"
  — "to qualify for admission to an advanced technical training program"
- course goals — "to develop drafting skills to a beginning commercial level"
  — "to adjust and replace auto brakes and maintain and repair hydraulic brake systems"
- personal goals — "to develop effective listening and note-taking skills"
  — "to find my own part-time job"

Goals are general statements about desired outcomes. They have an important psychological effect on our behavior whether we reach them or not, for they provide a focus for personal improvement and development. In that sense alone, it could be argued that in the very process of setting a goal a handicapped individual has already begun to make progress toward it.

Objectives are more specific, tend to be directly measurable, and in most instances pertain to activities of shorter duration. In an earlier section, attention was given to the IEP as a planning document: In the IEP, educational objectives are listed for each handicapped student in accordance with test findings and the consensus of IEP committee opinion. Thus, through the use of the IEP, school personnel, the parent, and the student should already be in agreement regarding important educational objectives toward which the student should be making progress. In most instances, the statement of an objective as written on an IEP will relate to basic skills, e.g. reading, speaking, mathematics, or to developmental skills, e.g. increase attention span, improve personal/social behavior, improve mobility skills.

As a member of the instructional staff, the vocational educator should be concerned with these IEP objectives and, of course, take primary responsibility when IEP objectives are stated in vocational terms.

It has also been pointed out that, because the scope of the IEP frequently falls short of establishing adequate course objectives, these will need to be developed by the individual instructors who implement the IEP. Some school districts have developed a companion document to be used by receiving teachers (those teachers with whom the handicapped student will be taking classes).

While the content of this latter instructional planning document will vary considerably from district to district and course to course, it should generally contain the following:

- short-term objectives (or goals) that are set cooperatively by the vocational educator and student, and with which the special educator should agree;
- a time line for when interim progress will be evaluated;
- brief statements describing (a) particular instruction techniques to be used and (b) special resources required;
- modifications in the course content and criteria for grading, facilities, etc. that may affect the achievement of the objectives or goals.

The format for the individualized instructional planning document need not be elaborate. Figure 12 shows an example drawn from *A Five County Vocational Skills Training Program for the Blind (1972)*, an informative project document prepared by Gene Russell for the Santa Cruz (California) County Office of Education.

When a handicapped student has been mainstreamed into a regular vocational class, the vocational educator and the special educator should especially consider the use of *interim objectives* toward which the student can work over a three- to six-week time span. The principal benefit to be derived from this strategy is that it allows (or, more correctly, requires) an interim evaluation of whether student needs are being met and whether instructional procedures are appropriate or in need of revision.

DESIGNING LEARNING CONTRACTS AND INSTRUCTIONAL MODULES

Previously, a rationale was presented for developing course content on the basis of job and task analysis, then compared to the unique qualities (both strengths and weaknesses) of the handicapped student as indicated by the IEP and by vocational evaluation. The need to cooperatively decide on learning objectives and goals that will be meaningful and useful to the student was also indicated.

Many options exist, of course, as to how vocational subject matter can be presented.

Johnson and Johnson (1970) have listed (and described) some twenty-five general methods of instruction, including the following:

1. comparative analysis
2. conference
3. demonstration
4. diagnosis
5. directed observation
6. discussion
7. drill
8. experimentation
9. field experience
10. field trips
11. group work
12. laboratory experience
13. lecture
14. manipulative tactile activity
15. modeling and imitation
16. problem solving
17. programmed instruction
18. project
19. reading
20. recitation
21. role play
22. seminar
23. sensitivity training
24. shopwork
25. skill practice sessions

INSTRUCTIONAL OBJECTIVES

Program: *Vocational Skills Training* Date: *January 21, 1972*

Pupil's Name: *Charles D. Hammer** Age: *17*

General Pupil Information:
Charles' vision impairment is due to congenital cataracts. His right eye has only light perception, while vision in the left eye is 5/100.

Instructional Goals:
1. Develop problem-solving abilities related to the materials, processes, and products of woodworking.
2. Develop skill in the safe use of tools and machines.
3. Develop skills in communication and sociability.

Instructional Objectives:
1. At the end of the semester, Charles will understand the following major concepts and information concerning woodworking:

a. Joints
b. Turning
c. Finishing
d. Hand Tool Identification, Use, and Care
e. Sawing
f. Boring
g. Shaping

Charles's understanding will be reflected in his receiving not less than a B grade in the class.

2. By the end of the semester, Charles will be able to operate unassisted the following pieces of equipment, performing at least one operation with each, and throughout the semester, without causing bodily injury to himself or his classmates:

a. Lathe
b. Drill Press
c. Mitre Saw
d. Jointer
e. Radial Saw
f. Surface Planer
g. Table Saw

3. By the end of the year, Charles will be able to independently ask for and offer assistance to other students 10 times to increase his sociability within a group.

**Fictitious name* Teacher ______________________

Figure 12. Instructional objectives planning form. (From the Santa Cruz County Office of Education, and Gene Russell.)

Although overlapping in some respects ("shopwork," for example, is an oversimplification that overlaps "demonstration," "manipulative/tactile," "project," and "skill practice sessions"), these categories can be helpful reminders of some of the more commonly used instructional approaches. Many of them can be effectively used in implementing individualized learning in the vocational classroom or lab. What is needed, however, is a practical means for matching methods of instruction to each of the objectives or goals toward which the student is working. One especially promising means for accomplishing this is the development of *instructional modules and learning contracts.*

The *instructional module* shown in Figure 13 is adapted from Phelps's (1976) helpful resource book on implementing vocational education for the handicapped. Beginning with an occupational area (decided through job market analysis), the excerpt names a specific task (identified by task analysis), states

CLUSTER/PROGRAM: Automotive TASK: Clean and adjust spark plugs

LEARNER: *Matt*

Progress: Introduced	Involved	Productive	Employable	Occupational Performance Objectives
				Given the necessary tools, materials, equipment, and requisite knowledge, the learner will: 1. Pick up and place plug in solvent solution. 2. Remove and place plug in plug holder jig with bottom up. 3. Wire brush until clean (use cleaned condition picture for comparison). 4. Determine plug gap by using different sized gauges and placing them between the gap until appropriate size is located. 5. Determine whether plug gap is correct by comparing gauge size with the master size on the poster attached to the bench. 6. If necessary, close gap by tapping the ground of the plug lightly with a soft-face hammer until the gap gauge is movable within the gap, but both the electrode and ground are touching the surface of the gap gauge. 7. Remove plug from jig and place in inspection basket.

Progress: Introduced	Developing	Competent	Basic Skills/Concepts	Basic Skills/Concept Content
			Finger dexterity	Grasp and hold spark plug.
			Form discrimination	Recognize electrode (top) and ground (bottom) ends of spark plug.
			Hand-eye coordination	Brushing strokes.
			Number recognition	.025, .030, .035, .040 (sizes on the various gauges).
			Number recognition and matching	Match 3-digit numbers shown above with those on a wall chart.
			Grasping	Hammer handle
			Fine motor coordination; manual dexterity	Light tapping of hammer on metal.
			Touch discrimination	Feeling the distances between metal surfaces by placing a metal plug between the surfaces
			Grasp and remove	

Figure 13. Excerpt of sample instructional module.

the performance objective in functional terms (specific activities the student must perform to accomplish the objective), identifies the key skills or concepts involved (perceptual, motor, intellectual, etc.), and provides a convenient checklist for evaluating student progress.

The language used for the progress ratings is clear and informative and can readily show the student's progress over time. In effect, this portion of the module states the "what" and the "how" (that is, the product and procedure) that signify competence in the task. It is important to note that *all* of the content in the Figure 13 example is *equally applicable* to handicapped and nonhandicapped persons.

In the second planning document, the *learning contract,* the instructional focus should be tailored to reflect individual differences. There are two main elements to the learning contract. The first portion states the instructor's responsibilities and resources to be used vis á vis that particular student. The second portion states the student's responsibilities and expectations insofar as they can be anticipated. Figure 14 continues to refer to the cleaning and adjustment of spark plugs, but shows the learning contract portion of the module.

The specifics of any learning contract will vary with the learning objectives, the individual, and the overall scope of the tasks involved. In the abbreviated example shown in Figure 14, the task was a small one, the kind of short-term "project" that is especially appropriate early in the course when the student's needs and abilities are still being determined. For some students (such as the mentally retarded) learning contracts may continue to be short and simple, while for other students it should be possible to gradually expand the scope of the contract to encompass a much larger set of tasks.

It is appropriate to keep in mind that *attitudes* are an important element of instruction for the handicapped. While attention rightfully should be focused on the student's performance (skills and work habits), there should be a conscious effort to work toward building positive attitudes in those first few weeks. Moreover, building positive attitudes should be a

LEARNING CONTRACT

TASK: *Clean and adjust spark plugs*

SCHEDULE: *two hours* CRITERION: *4 different plugs ok'd.*

INSTRUCTOR RESPONSIBILITIES:

1. *Demonstrate each step so that the student can see it.*
2. *Guide the student's hands for step 4 (sizing) and step 6 (tapping)*
3. *Check student's knowledge of three-digit numbers. Provide extra help on step 5 when the chart is used.*
4. *Use verbal reinforcement for each correct plug.*
5. *Build a jig to hold the spark plug in an inverted position.*

STUDENT RESPONSIBILITIES:

1. *Clean and set plug #1 by following each step as it is demonstrated.*
2. *Clean and set plug #2 with no more than one question or assistance.*
3. *Clean and set plug #3 independently and correctly.*
4. *Clean and set plug #4 as quickly as possible, then record time in your notebook. The plug must be correct for the time to count.*

OTHER AGREEMENTS:

Punch in and out of lab on the time clock.

INCENTIVE: *Opportunity to clean plugs in own car*

SIGNED: ______________________________ *(Instructor)*
SIGNED: ______________________________ *(Student)*

Figure 14. Learning contract portion of an individualized module.

common goal for the handicapped student, nonhandicapped peers in the class, and the instructor.

Many variations of individualized instructional modules and learning contracts are possible, of course, but the format developed within a given vocational training center or school district should consistently permit (1) instructor and student responsibilities to be spelled out in advance, (2) learning objectives to be evaluated simply and efficiently, and (3) evaluation to be linked directly to student performance in each of the significant task elements and/or tasks within a job competency.

OVERCOMING BARRIERS TO INSTRUCTION

Planning and implementing an individualized vocational education program are, in a very real sense, dependent upon the subject matter (knowledge, skills, and habits) to be learned and upon the capabilities and interests of the student. They are also dependent upon barriers that may need to be overcome if the student is to be benefitted in a significant way. Typically, these barriers have been thought of as problems of facility or equipment access, problems of visual or aural communication, and problems of transportation or mobility. Less frequently, but still of major importance, are attitudinal barriers, which all too often limit the opportunities that are made available to the handicapped.

Dahl, Appleby, and Lipe (1978) have extensively analyzed the barriers confronting handicapped persons in vocational classes. They have categorized problems according to four major areas of demand placed on the handicapped person, including (1) physical demands, (2) visual demands, (3) auditory and speech demands, and (4) intellectual demands. For any given student, barriers may exist in one or more of these areas, they may exist in varying degrees, and there may be different ways of overcoming or eliminating those barriers in whole or in part.

As indicated previously, Section 504 of the Rehabilitation Act has directed national attention toward removal of any barriers that unfairly discriminate against the handicapped whether at school, on the job, or in the community. The primary concern of the vocational educator/special educator instructional team will be to identify barriers that can and should be overcome in relation to a particular student and identify modifications or alternatives that will involve minimum cost and disruption to the educational program or work site. Keeping the costs of barrier removal down not only makes good economic sense but also is likely to lead to the quickest, most practical barrier removal.

Modifications to equipment are an obvious area of concern to vocational educators although even these changes are not always necessary or even desirable. They tend to occur less frequently than one might imagine, in part because of the adaptive abilities and resourcefulness of many handicapped persons.

Dahl, Appleby and Lipe (1978) proposed three strategies or choices over which the vocational educator has some control, especially in connection with the use of vocational equipment. They include the following:

1. *Selecting standard equipment that has been designed in such a way that it can be readily used by the handicapped.* Examples are numerous, with only a few being cited below.
   — The Weller Electric Soldering Gun cools so quickly that work can be positioned by fingertip by the blind with only a minimum delay.
   — The Gestetner Offset Duplicator Model SEM 319 has been simplified and automated to facilitate its use by various handicapped persons. By using illuminated symbols on the control panel and other visual cueing techniques, the machine has been made suitable for use by the deaf. By using levers and wings (in place of knobs), automatic paper feeds, automatic wash of the printing blanket, "fingerless" attachment of the printing plate to the cylinder, and a low mobile stand, the machine can readily be used by a wide variety of neurologically or orthopedically handicapped persons.
   — The Magna Wonder Knife has a slicing guide attached to the blade. By adjusting a thumb screw, blind persons can slice foods consistently to any desired thickness.
   — The Stanley Adjustable Mitre Saw allows angle cuts to be made cleanly and precisely by persons with low vision or poor motor coordination.
2. *Provide the student with an aid or with specially designed equipment.* Examples include
   — a magnifier that a visually handicapped person could freely position above a work area or affix to equipment

such as a drillpress. Magnifiers can be hand held (Kaiser) or free standing (Electro-Optix), and with or without built-in illuminators.

— a keyboard template that a poorly coordinated person could place on a typewriter to avoid mistakenly hitting keys.

— a Starrett micrometer with braille markings to enable blind persons to carry out precision measurements, or a telescoping click rule that can be pre-set to measure specific distances.

— a Manual Communications Module (consisting of a portable keyboard, visual panel, and telephone coupling), which allows deaf persons to use the telephone while "on-the-road," or which can be used by sighted persons wishing to communicate with the deaf remotely or communicate in person when signing or speech reading is not possible.

3 . *Modify existing equipment as necessary to make it usable.* Examples include

— adding raised marks to heavy-duty equipment by using solder or drops of white glue to enable the blind to determine settings.

— adding levers or rubber grips to facilitate turning of knobs and handles by orthopedically handicapped persons.

— adding visual meters for the deaf or audible meters for the blind to enable readings of gas or electric equipment.

— removing braces under tables and/or raising table height to allow wheelchair access; lowering cabinets where materials are kept; and providing safety guards where individuals could be exposed to equipment hazards.

In the limited number of examples given above it is clear that advance planning at the time of equipment purchase can do much to hold down costs for later modification. Some minor expenses in adapting equipment can be anticipated, but by using common sense these adjustments can often be minimized.

Hopefully, the special educator and the vocational educator

can strike a balance between the purchase of specialized equipment (such as a "talking" calculator), carrying out simple modifications (such as adding colored cues to equipment to guide the mentally retarded as they perform a sequence of steps), or selecting more appropriate tools (such as using a pressure lock wrench to grasp and turn a nut or knob). It is worth being restated that the low-cost solution is frequently the best one, not only because it is economical but also because it is usually quickly implemented and, therefore, will be the most likely way that a handicapped person could accomplish the task in a variety of settings in the future.

Figure 15 provides a checklist for analyzing needed equipment changes to remove barriers. It is intended to focus attention on the less elaborate, more broadly useful barrier removal options.

The instructional team should keep in mind that similar procedures can be applied to environmental barriers and transportation barriers as well as to equipment that is used on the job. They should also realize that job re-engineering is another form of barrier removal. In the classroom this can mean having a specific subtask done by someone else, while on the job it could mean redefining the job responsibilities or even changing the way the job is performed.

The key to appropriate modification of the classroom environment rests in constructing a total picture of the individual, the process, and the interfacing mechanisms that are minimally necessary to allow the individual to perform the essential tasks. Note that the *last* step is the use of assistive or special devices. This is true because the preferred, and lower cost, solutions to the reductions of barriers involve altered work assignments and the learning of new techniques. Put another way, if the individual can be taught a new way of doing something, or can learn a "shortcut" that avoids the problem altogether, it is much preferred to the introduction of additional hardware. On the other hand, special equipment that will be used repeatedly is often a very effective solution, and the handicapped individual should be entitled to that type of help whenever it is really beneficial. Needless to say, decisions about the most appropriate approach to barrier removal are best made at the local

TASK: *Thread sewing machine*

HANDICAP(S): *Visually handicapped (blind)*

Specify Major Steps	Seeing	Hearing	Speaking	Handling	Lifting	Reaching	Other	Teach new method	Adapt equipment	Buy new device	Other help	Ok as is
#1. *Select thread*	*X*			*X*		*X*		*X*				
#2. *Mount spool*				*X*		*X*						*X*
#3. *Thread guide*				*X*								*X*
#4. *Thread needle*	*X*			*X*						*X*		
#5. *Etc.*												

Possible instructional changes not requiring added expense:

Use braille coding on various colored spools.

Possible equipment modifications at minimum expense:

None.

Possible devices to purchase at modest expense:

Buy self-threading needle or needle threader from the American Foundation for the Blind.

Figure 15. Barrier analysis and modification planning sheet.

level where individual cases can be considered.

If questions about barrier removal arise that cannot be answered locally, it may be appropriate to telephone or write the National Center for a Barrier Free Environment, Washington, D.C. This organization can provide technical advice specific to a problem, provide resource packets dealing with specific architectural problems such as kitchen design, or carry out customized information searches in response to inquiries.

Earlier, mention was made of the importance of planning ahead to the time when the handicapped student would be seeking employment in the community. A serious barrier encountered by many handicapped persons is getting to and from the work site. Approaches to the resolution of this problem will vary considerably with the type of handicap, of course, but it is quite likely that it will arise as a problem for the visually handicapped and blind, the mentally retarded, the deaf who have not developed confidence in dealing with the hearing, and especially with the orthopedically handicapped. In recent years there has been increasing attention to the inadequacies of public transportation to serve this latter group, and many of them have been able to circumvent this problem with specially adapted private automobiles. The visually handicapped have also begun to qualify more and more frequently as drivers due to special procedures initiated in some states for establishing their safe driving limits.

The Veterans Administration has had a leading role in the adaptation of automobiles to serve the handicapped and is a useful source of information. Among the recent and helpful publications on the subject are the following:

> *The Handicapped Driver's Mobility Guide.* American Automobile Association, 1978. Includes modification suggestions and a state-by-state listing of organizations that can help in some way.
>
> *Hand Controls and Assistive Devices for the Physically Disabled Driver.* Human Resources Center, Albertson, NY, 1977. Includes descriptions and photographs of various adaptive devices and hand controls, together with criteria for appropriate selection.
>
> *Accent On Living Buyer's Guide.* Accent Special Publications, Cheever Publications, Bloomington, IL, 1978. A comprehensive guide with a useful section on automobile travel, controls, and aids.

If it appears that the student will need an adapted automobile for his or her employment the Department of Rehabilitation may help with the cost.

EVALUATING INSTRUCTIONAL OUTCOMES

There is no doubt that the measurement of outcomes is important — important to the student, the instructor, the eventual employer, and important from the standpoint of good educational practice and legal requirements. In the latter regard, Public Law 94-142 requires the evaluation, at least annually, of the extent to which the objectives in the handicapped student's individualized educational program have been met. Even if this evaluation were not mandated, it is highly desirable that the handicapped student's performance should be evaluated carefully for school purposes. This is especially true where the handicapped student is mainstreamed with nonhandicapped students, for this information can affect subsequent placement of the student as well as educational programming in that class.

Certainly if it was evident at the end of a course that the student had had a very positive experience, this would point to the probable viability of participation by other similarly handicapped students. Suppose, on the other hand, that the overall appraisal of outcomes led to conclusions that the student had gained little and had, on several occasions, been at risk because there had been consistent difficulty in following safety guidelines. In such a case, there might be good reason to avoid similar student assignments *until and unless* these deficiencies could be corrected by the instructional staff and administration. This does not justify inaction but rather implies that special effort is needed, perhaps using supplemental vocational education funds to make necessary equipment or facility modifications or to make other changes.

As has already been pointed out, the evaluation of training outcomes is of central importance to both the student and the employer. It is important to the sense of worth of the handicapped student to know that he or she has gained new skills, developed new patterns of behavior, and has the potential to be productively employed. Training outcomes are particularly important to the employer because the more clearly stated are the handicapped student's strengths *and* weaknesses the more practical it becomes to hire the student. This sounds somewhat contradictory, but it really is not. In effect, it means that the employer can more clearly determine what parts of the job may be done by the handicapped person and which should be done by another employee. This saves time and money that might have been expended in experimentation and frustration. It also means that the employer will be in a better position to determine a fair wage, perhaps equal to that of other beginning employees or perhaps at a lowered rate as agreed to with regulatory agencies.

Assessment of outcomes should be complete and expressed in terms of the student's

- specific skills and subskills, including the quality of performance demonstrated
- work habits and attitudes, including reliability, punctuality, and other important job-related factors
- interpersonal and social relationships that might bear upon job performance.

To illustrate, suppose a mentally retarded student had recently completed a food service class (conducted in connection with the school's cafeteria) and was now being considered for employment by the owner of a small coffee shop. Suppose too that the student was able to bus tables and serve food as had been expected, but in addition had learned how to make change, thereby surprising the instructional staff. This is the kind of information that any employer would certainly want to know, and might make the difference in whether the student was hired. That is not to say that the student would be a plausible choice to do all the cashiering in the coffee shop, but rather that it might be helpful to have a backup if the coffee shop's cashier is temporarily unavailable.

What is being argued for, then, is a straightforward reporting of student's competencies in terms that are meaningful to employers. Figure 16 is an abbreviated example of such a competency report.

The following discussion makes clear that the evaluation of outcomes accomplishes a number of purposes. First, it is mandated that the individualized educational program be annually reviewed. Second, it is a good way to establish the overall "workability" of the course for handicapped persons, pointing out problems that await administrative solution or the

Student: SJ	Class: Retail bakery	School: Jones	1978

SKILLS AREAS

1. Food preparation: (a) mixes dough, (b) bakes cookies, (c) decorates baked goods
   a. can proportion the ingredients according to written instructions
   b. uses sizing equipment and timer
   c. applies icing, rosettes, lettering (simple)
   Quality of performance: SJ clearly enjoys cookie preparation and is creative with the decoration of baked goods, though still new at it.
2. Customer Service: (a) boxes and delivers items, (b) makes change, (c) waits on customers
   a. properly loads boxes and ties string around them, makes deliveries to nearby customers
   b. has made change on several occasions when special bake sales have taken place
   c. does not easily understand the wide range of customers' requests, but usually does not need help
3. Clean Up: (a) cleans mixing bowls, and (b) display racks
4. (Etc.)

WORK HABITS

1. Consistently punctual, willing to work late if necessary.
2. Follows safety precautions around mixers and oven.
3. Still needs training on how to use time clocks or time cards since these were not taught.
4. (Etc.)

ATTITUDES AND INTERPERSONAL RELATIONSHIPS

1. Very cooperative when given assignments, will come frequently to ask advice if not sure.
2. Has made several friends among delivery customers, who ask about his (her) whereabouts when someone else delivers.
3. Needs to build confidence when waiting on customers at counter.
4. (Etc.)

Figure 16. A hypothetical student's competency report, an outcome evaluation prepared for use with prospective employers.

teacher's revision if the course is to be made more effective for other handicapped students yet to come. Third, evaluation of outcomes is of great importance to the student, a way of acknowledging achievements (however large or small they might be), and of great importance to any prospective employer, a way of listing developed competencies in terms that are meaningful in the world of work.

TEAMWORK IN INSTRUCTIONAL IMPLEMENTATION

Role definition is essential if the vocational educator and special educator are to be effective in support of the student. Instructional interaction with the student rests with the vocational educator, of course, as do the many day-to-day judgments that are a part of the instructional process. Thus, the special educator plays a subordinate, supportive role (but by no means an unimportant one) once the decision has been made that the handicapped student should participate in vocational education.

The quality of support the special education teacher can provide will be much enhanced if he or she becomes better acquainted with the occupational subject matter being taught and with the processes that the student must be able to master if he or she is to develop job-ready skills.

To illustrate, a class in ornamental horticulture rather obviously calls for a number of manipulative skills such as seeding, watering, fertilizing, repotting, and pruning. However, if the seeding process is examined in greater detail it is immediately apparent that more is required of the student than the simple insertion of seeds into soil. Thus, the student may reasonably be expected to learn new vocabulary, including such words as vermiculite, saturate, germination, environment, drainage, and the name of the plant. Measurement will also be required in terms of depth of planting, amount of watering, and ideal temperature level. The special educator could coordinate the student's study of the vocabulary and math with other teachers, or, if that would not be practical, could provide personal or temporary tutorial assistance as needed.

Special educators should also play a key role in helping the vocational educator to specify appropriate learning objectives for each student, suggest alternative ways in which tasks could be accomplished by the handicapped person, and become directly involved in adapting instructional techniques, materials and equipment, or the instructional setting. The special educator/vocational educator team should maintain a flexible, creative stance with respect to the provision of personalized assistance, adaptive techniques, and special resources. Figure 17 illustrates a few of the options.

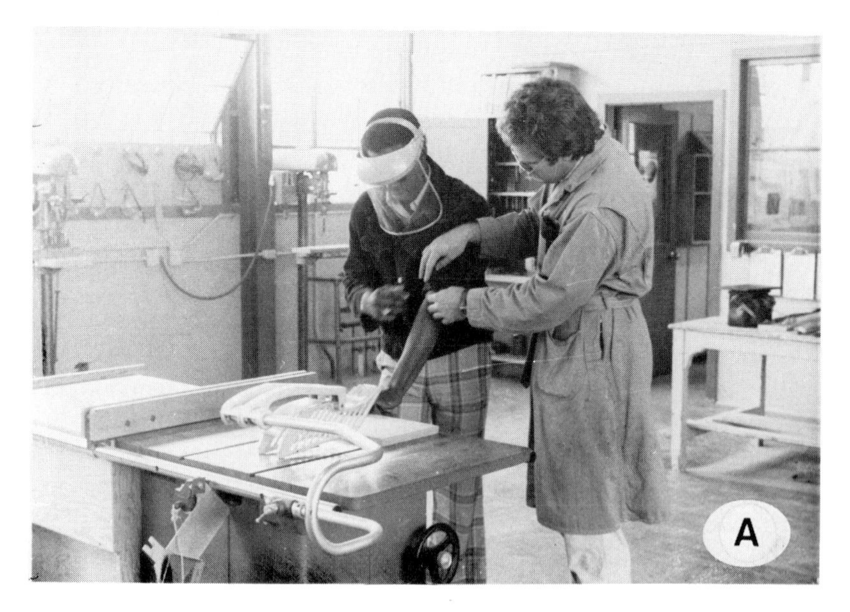

Figure 17. Forms of special assistance for handicapped students. A. Personalized instruction by the teacher. B. "Buddy system" or other temporary help.

C. Special purpose devices and audiovisual media. D. Adaptive techniques for performing tasks.

In review, the planning of curricula and the implementation of instruction involve a number of steps and considerations. These include a careful study of the job market, task analysis, comparison with the particular handicapped student's strengths and limitations, and design and development of appropriate instructional modules and learning contracts. A team approach is required, with the vocational educator and special educator each contributing in complementary ways as suggested below.

GOAL	SPECIAL EDUCATOR FUNCTION	VOCATIONAL EDUCATOR FUNCTION
Prescribe an appropriate program of studies	Establish role of vocational instruction within overall educational programming	Analyze job/task requirements in terms of the individual's profile
	Specify indicators of progress and points at which program planning should be re-evaluated	Review curriculum in terms of "required" and "optional" assignments and procedures.
	Suggest alternative techniques and strategies.	Plan adaptive instruction
		Modify expectations regarding task/time allocations
Design barrier-free learning environment	Assure access to the vocational training facility	Devise alternative procedures
	Identify or supply resources, supplemental aid, and special devices	Arrange room furniture and/or modify equipment at instructional station.
	Provide follow-up support and advice on as-needed basis	Revise means for storing and/or identification of parts and supplies.
		Involve nonhandicapped students constructively.

PART III

THE TRANSITION FROM SCHOOL TO WORK AND INDEPENDENT LIVING

CHAPTER 7

PROBLEMS AND POTENTIALS

SOMEONE once said that the prettiest flowers grow in the deepest part of the woods. In other words, they may be more difficult to acquire, but they are apt to be worth the extra effort. So it is with a large proportion of the handicapped, for though they may have special problems that require adaptive effort they tend to be among the more valued employees in a firm once they have had those problems resolved.

Illustrative of some of the problems faced by the handicapped is a "needs assessment" survey conducted by Doctor Leonard Perlman and summarized in the National Epilepsy League's 1977 publication, *The Person With Epilepsy . . . Life Style, Needs, Expectations*. Consider, for example, these quotes from two of the 363 randomly selected survey respondents, all of whom had epilepsy.

1. "The only jobs I ever got were the ones that I didn't tell about my epilepsy."
2. "We can deal with epilepsy, but our problem exists with people who are uneducated toward the disease. Employers are even scared of the word *epilepsy*."

Epilepsy has indeed been one of the handicapping conditions most avoided by employers over the years. This prejudice was reaffirmed in the Perlman survey results, for "discrimination in jobs" was rated as the *most serious problem* facing persons with epilepsy. Fully 50 percent of those surveyed stated that epilepsy had created problems in obtaining a job and 51 percent stated that epilepsy was the reason for their unemployment.

In contrast, of those surveyed epileptics who were fully employed, 75 percent said their employers knew of their epilepsy and 67 percent felt that it was important that the employer know about the condition. For example, although epileptic seizures can be controlled through medication in over half the cases, this fact is not fully appreciated by employers. This does not mean that an epileptic's problems necessarily disappear when the individual is on a program of medication, for the medication itself can cause side effects that should be taken into account when assigning job duties. Thus, drowsiness (the most common side effect) should not be taken by an employer as an indication of laziness on the job. Nor should an assignment be made that would put the employee at risk if the second most frequent side effect, dizziness, is recognized. These are little more than common sense adjustments and by no means suggest that the individual would be unable to function effectively as an employee.

Fortunately, the picture is not all negative. A number of employers have come to realize that handicapped workers are worth seeking out. For example, Joyce Hubbs, a supervisor in the Academy of Health Sciences, United States Army, states that "handicapped operators in my word processing center have increased productivity, improved morale, and have been invaluable in the total operation" (Hantman, 1977). Lucille Townsend, a word processing supervisor in the Department of Agriculture, adds the comment that "the fast typing speed of a deaf operator sets the tempo for the center and subconsciously the other operators try to keep up with it." Dottie Carter, from the United States Army Surgeon General's Office, goes even further in her praise. "I'd hire the handicapped, no matter what their disability. They'd be so happy to have a job, they'd be my best workers. If I could do it all over again, I'd have all handicapped operators."

Interestingly, this positive experience is not a recent phenomenon in the federal government, and it holds true for a wide range of handicapping conditions. In 1969, the Civil Service Commission surveyed the progress of some 391 persons who were severely handicapped and had entered government service through special appointment, thereby bypassing the inequities of employment opportunity that would have eliminated them if had they taken the competitive examinations designed for the ablebodied. Following are some of the highlights of the Civil Service Commission findings for these individuals, more than half of whom were multiply handicapped (Love, 1971).

- Contrary to the general assumption, 80 percent of the employees required no change in the work site. Where changes were made they were mainly centered on the rearranging of desks and file cabinets, adding a ramp at an access door, etc.
- The overwhelming majority were rated "excellent" or "normal" by their supervisors on (a) how well they followed direction, (b) relations to co-workers and the supervisors themselves, and (c) general job performance. Only five of the nearly 400 persons who had been appointed under this waiver program had been separated from employment as a result of unsatisfactory ratings.
- If one discounts the 100 appointees who had served less than a year and, therefore, were ineligible for promotion, of the remainder surveyed, some 48 percent had received one or more promotions within a five-year period. Moreover, the supervisors answered yes in 231 instances, as against no in 137 instances, when asked whether the appointees had definite promise for assignment to more responsible duties.
- The jobs were varied in type, spanning some 88 job categories, and ranged from the general helper and box-maker level positions to physicist and mathematician. However, the majority of the opportunities were at the entry level.

EMPLOYERS' DOUBTS AND POSSIBLE ANSWERS

It is understandable that employers who have not had the experience of working with handicapped persons will be skeptical of the impact that such a person will have in their business. Studies have been conducted by a number of firms to establish the pros and cons of employing the handicapped, with interesting results. The du Pont Company, with over 1,400 handicapped employees, conducted a survey throughout its organizations, found its handicapped employees were exemplary, subsequently stepped up its recruitment of the handicapped, and has since encouraged other firms to follow suit. Hewlett-Packard, Fairchild, and other major electronics firms on the West Coast have similarly concluded that the handicapped should be sought out because they are capable and reliable.

The following listing, adapted from Sinick (1969), summarizes the objections that employers raise and suggest some appropriate responses, including some that would surprise many employers.

Objection	*Response*
1. Productivity is lower.	1. It has been shown to equal or exceed the unimpaired.
2. Turnover is higher.	2. There is a greater loyalty, and much less turnover.
3. Absenteeism is greater.	3. There is less absenteeism, plus more punctuality and dependability.
4. There are more accidents.	4. There are less accidents, and fewer accidents are severe.
5. Workmen's compensation rates rise.	5. Rates are lowered, if anything, due to fewer accidents.
6. Total disability liability is greater.	6. Second injury funds maintained by many states reduce this liability.
7. Health and insurance costs rise.	7. Rates are based on sex and age, not handicap.
8. There are higher overall costs.	8. Changing disabled persons from tax-recipients to productive taxpayers could reduce taxes.
9. Physical plant is not appropriate.	9. Changes are generally possible and at less cost than imagined.
10. Medical examinations screen out applicants.	10. Medical examinations often include information not related to the performance of the job.
11. The union won't hire them.	11. Union literature favors such hirings.
12. Supervisors and co-workers won't approve.	12. After adjustment, the handicapped worker is found to improve morale and is valued.
13. Customers won't approve.	13. Improved public relations can result

Objection	*Response*
	for the employer, due in part to the observed loyalty of the employees and evidence of their ability.
14. The disabled are emotional and disagreeable.	14. Attractive personalities are found among the handicapped as among the nonhandicapped.
15. They need special consideration.	15. They generally avoid asking for favors or special allowance.
16. They are limited to low-level jobs.	16. They are successful at all levels.
17. Adaptability to different jobs is hampered.	17. Individualized placement will avoid mismatched jobs.
18. Firing or layoff is difficult.	18. Regular personnel policy should apply.
19. We already have enough handicapped.	19. Then you should be aware of how effective they can be.
20. We have other sources of applicants.	20. This additional source can work to your advantage.
21. We prefer people who find their own jobs.	21. Nonhandicapped persons often use placement services.
22. We avoid government placement agencies.	22. We are not regulatory and the service is free to you.
23. You aren't familiar with our operations.	23. Request a plant tour and orientation.
24. Why experiment with us?	24. No experiment is intended since the abilities of the handicapped have repeatedly been proven across the country.

Of course, the issues and answers presented above cannot anticipate all the possible "problems" that can be raised, nor do they reflect the particulars that might apply in a given case. As has already been pointed out, however, Section 504 of the Rehabilitation Act effectively precludes discrimination in hiring. This certainly adds substantial weight to the rational responses that have been suggested in the preceding list.

Individual Success Stories and Personal Achievements

The newly enlightened atmosphere concerning the handicapped includes a reversal of pattern in the media. Formerly eschewing coverage of the handicapped as being unnewsworthy, there is now a nearly constant flow of information about their achievements. Some are occupational in nature, some are related to homemaking and independent living, and some are exhilarating examples of persistence in physical activities or leisure pursuits. For illustrative purposes a variety of ages, occupations, and achievements are included in the vignettes that follow.

- Bonnie Consuelo is a fully functioning homemaker, though she has no arms. The educational film "A Day in the Life of Bonnie Consuelo" is totally convincing. It shows her driving to the market, selecting vegetables, signing a check (with her toes) at the checkout counter, cooking, serving, eating, cleaning up, and fulfilling numerous other daily duties.
- Vivian Younger is in her mid twenties, boasts a perfect 4.0 grade point average in graduate school, has a bowling average of 110, runs the mile in six minutes, and is loved by her students, whether she's strumming the guitar or leading gym class. Blind since birth, she says "its a nuisance, that's all."
- Kathy O'Neil is deaf as well as slight in build. These are hardly the qualifications that one expects of a person engaged in activities where sounds can make a critical difference, like setting speed records of over 500 miles per hour on land, or performing spectacular stunts in Hollywood.
- Harry Cordellos received a state commendation for his effectiveness in telling others how to get from place to place in his role as information officer. Though blind, he reads the necessary printed material with an electronic device, and on his off-duty hours pursues jogging, golfing, bowling, swimming, and water skiing.
- Elaine Naismith, stewardess, adds beauty and grace to United Airlines' service between San Francisco and New York.

An amputee, her artificial leg does not decrease her effectiveness on the job, and it does not stop her from having fun on the tennis court.

- David Michalowski skated beautifully through a complicated routine during the nationally televised 1978 United States Figure Skating Championships, keeping in close harmony with recorded music he could not hear. Aided by hand signals from his coach, the twenty year old acknowledged the judges' high marks by clapping along with the audience.
- Dan O'Hara is a crusader for better programs and facilities for the disabled through his Handicapped Awareness Foundation. That does not mean that Dan wants things easy. If he did he would hardly be likely to enter cross-country "foot" races in his wheelchair, or propel himself tediously across the Golden Gate Bridge and along highways enroute to the state capitol to lobby for his ideas.
- Curt Landtroop learned as a blind child to compete with sighted children by developing an independent style of problem solving, such as riding a two-wheel bike alone and fast by guiding himself with the depression along the curb. Having lived through an exciting childhood, Curt leads an exciting adult life, using special braille computer equipment to manage and invest some $50 to $150 million dollars a day for General Motors.
- Celestine Tate took her case to court and won it. To the court's satisfaction, she demonstrated that she is a fit mother, able to care for her infant child's basic needs (including the changing of diapers) even though Celestine herself is limbless.
- Sondra Diamond has become an inspiring and skilled public speaker on behalf of the handicapped in spite of the serious speech impairment and physical problems that result from her cerebral palsied condition.

These examples are by no means exhaustive of the range of achievements of the handicapped, and really only emphasize that stereotypic thinking should be avoided when considering the kinds of adult roles that handicapped persons can fulfill.

Blindness, deafness, and orthopedic handicaps such as those cited previously are undoubtedly frustrating, yet they provide dramatic proofs about the payoffs of persistence and self-reliance. Other handicaps that are less apparent to the casual observer can nevertheless seriously impede the processing of information of a written or spoken nature. Thus, late Governor and Vice President Nelson Rockefeller gradually learned how to cope with a learning disability (in his case a visual perceptual problem) that made his schooling much more difficult than that of his peers. At a more popular level, Debra Clinger is a successful young actress who recently starred in a national television series. With a visual malfunction, dyslexia, Debra could not read scripts and had to memorize them. Now, working hard at overcoming her problem, she says, "I love books," which is quite a change for someone who could not take an IQ test because she could not read it.

No longer can it be assumed that persons with long-term handicaps will resign themselves to stereotyped "limited" jobs. Nor does the onset of a handicap necessarily mean that the person is no longer capable of doing what he or she was successful in before. After all, Beethoven was an accomplished pianist and composer *before* he became deaf, but his *greatest* compositions (the Third *Eroica* Symphony, the extremely popular Fifth Symphony, the Sixth *Pastoral* Symphony, the Fifth *Emperor* Piano Concerto, and the *Fidelio Opera*) were written during a period when his hearing was sharply impaired. His productivity continued (the Ninth *Missa Solemnis* Symphony and five string quartet compositions) even after he was totally deaf. Had Beethoven been "employed" as a composer, his employer might have laid him off or decided to "retrain" him into a more suitable line of work.

INDEPENDENT LIVING THROUGH COOPERATIVE EFFORT

Previously it has been stated that the handicapped generally prefer to be independent and involved in the mainstream of society to the maximum extent possible. This has been accomplished by some handicapped persons through their own cooperative effort. As an example, the Center for Independent Living, begun in 1972 in Berkeley, California, was started with the idea of making it possible for handicapped persons attending the University of California to live off campus, thereby learning self-reliance while they pursued their academic studies. The Center has grown considerably over the years until in 1978 it could claim some 117 staff members, the majority of whom were disabled.

Functioning much as a team, with shared duties and responsibilities, the success experienced by the Berkeley Center became an inspiration to other groups of handicapped persons throughout the state. In addition to the Berkeley Center, twelve other independent living centers have now begun in California alone. Each of the Centers helps its disabled participants through a peer modeling approach, in which those who can do things share their experiences with others, giving them the impetus to grow and begin to try things on their own. Collectively, the members of these centers take pride in demonstrating to nonhandicapped persons that they can indeed be active, contributing members of the community.

As one looks at the accomplishments of persons who, all too often, are thought of as "incapable," it becomes apparent that many have not been given opportunities to develop and demonstrate their capabilities. This calls for an interdisciplinary team effort on the part of *all* those who are in a position to make contructive inputs. Undeniably, vocational educators can play an important role in this regard, just as can special educators, physicians, psychologists, counselors, fellow students, and employers.

CHAPTER 8

WORK READINESS, JOB PLACEMENT, AND FOLLOW-UP

VOCATIONAL education, by definition, is intended to prepare the individual for entry into the world of work at some point. Just when this transition occurs is a function of school programming, student maturity and readiness, and the availability of opportunities in the job market. Within this framework, the special educator/vocational educator instructional team can help to bridge the gap between the priorities of instructors in an educational setting and the priorities of employers in business and industry. Links between school and business are especially important for the handicapped individual since lack of preparation, coordination, and follow-through is very likely to result in unemployment. As will be discussed more fully, school staff should work toward developing a strong, community-based educational program that leads to successful work placement for the handicapped. In many instances they will find this difficult to accomplish if their efforts are restricted by school budgets and school scheduling and, therefore, should coordinate their efforts with staff in the local office of the Department of Rehabilitation and staff in local service agencies organized to serve the handicapped.

ESTABLISHING QUALIFICATIONS FOR EMPLOYMENT

Work Exposure

In a programmatic sense, every handicapped student who has been receiving instruction in vocational classes, regardless of the occupational area, needs to be given a chance to apply newly learned skills in an actual work setting. The premise behind this statement is that a class in welding, machining, graphics, marine engines, dental assisting, or any of numerous other occupational areas is primarily intended to develop the student's knowledge, skills, and work habits within that subject matter up to a level of employability.

Considering an electronics class as an example, the course might be organized in such a way that it begins with principles, terminology, and information that is fundamental to work in the field. This is then followed by a series of exercises that are graduated in complexity and difficulty. These exercises help to (1) familiarize the student with a range of applications of the subject matter, e.g. receivers, detectors, (2) provide a limited amount of exposure to some of the tools, techniques, and skills involved, and (3) serve to help the student clarify the extent of his or her interest in the field. For the most part, success in these vocational classes is demonstrated through tests (cognitive, performance, or some combination thereof) or the "quality" of project products (which may or may not be of functional use, but which are generally not made for sale).

Increasingly, however, vocational educators are re-organizing their courses to more closely resemble a working environment as well as a study environment. One high school welding instructor in the San Jose (CA) city schools system has his students run a small business for fabricating, finishing, and marketing an extensive variety of decorative and functional items, e.g. metal trivets, plant containers. Deaf students in the class are finding that they are learning much more than a welding skill — they are learning teamwork, responsibility, good work habits, and at the same time they are developing a feeling of accomplishment and confidence that they can "make it" when they graduate.

Regional Occupation Programs, more frequently than high school vocational programs, offer classes in which instruction takes place in a joblike setting. Whether it is a bakery, auto body shop, office services, landscaping, or upholstering class, the tasks are often centered on products and processes that have direct commercial value. In many instances ROP programs are physically situated in a light industrial location with different classes operating in separate buildings, further adding to the businesslike rather than schoollike atmosphere. An emphasis on job placement, using well-established links with employers, characterizes many ROP programs. Because of this, ROP programs often closely reflect community work opportunities and are a highly appropriate channel to employment for the handicapped interested in the courses offered.

Work study, work experience, and cooperative education are three types of vocational education programs in which the "coursework" will normally involve off-campus activity in a business or industrial setting. These programs, frequently carried out on a districtwide level and using coordinators (or counselors) at each participating high school, provide practical opportunities for students who hope to be hired in the occupational field they are studying. In some situations, the coursework consists of short "surveys" of work experience, with students rotating through a series of short-term assignments, e.g. trying different jobs at a motel, such as foods preparation, food service, laundry and linens, front desk, housekeeping, and gardening. Somewhat more commonly, however, placement will extend over one quarter or one semester in a particular business establishment.

Depending on the type of educational program that has been organized, and local rules that may apply, many of these students are able to earn while they learn. That is, they will receive both pay and course credit. Perhaps even more important for handicapped students, they are being given a chance to prove their capabilities and worth both to their employers and to themselves. This self-awareness coupled with on-the-job experience can go a long way toward helping them find a job of their own.

Work Readiness

Previously, the importance of evaluation in establishing course outcomes has been mentioned. Instructor "certification," which describes the tasks and the level of proficiency developed during a course, is one very obvious and useful indicator of work readiness. When the course includes a component or phase in which the student reports to an employer or is judged on work performance by someone other than the instructor, a unique opportunity exists for evaluation of job readiness based on observational data.

Since observational data are subject to bias on the part of the rater or observer, it is increasingly common to find that the rating process is shared by several persons who interact with the student in terms of the characteristics being rated. In this way, different perceptions of the student's performance are brought to the surface, where they can be analyzed and taken into consideration when work placement is being considered.

Kaplan (1977) gives an interesting example of the use of comparative ratings to develop a student profile of job skills, attitudes, and self-concept. He includes a Student Profile filled out for a seventeen year old, mentally retarded high school junior participating in a work study program. While the profile is too lengthy and complex to be included here (it is 5 pages long and includes 9 sections) it is nevertheless deserving of inspection and consideration for possible adoption, in whole or in part.

Section one of the Student Profile developed by Kaplan is of particular interest. It provides space for comparative ratings by the student, the parent, the employer, the teacher, and the coordinator of work study on some thirty-five job skills and attitude dimensions and ten additional skills and activities revealing self-concept and influencing job performance. Further, the format for this rating process enables the evaluation of the student qualitatively (i.e., outstanding, good, fair, poor, failing), quantitatively (i.e., almost always, mostly, sometimes, rarely, almost never), or grossly (i.e., can hold a job, hold job?, cannot hold job) as appropriate for each of the dimensions.

In the case of the seventeen year old used as an example by Kaplan, it is interesting to note that the majority of the ratings fell centrally on the scale but that the student tended to be the most negative of the five persons whose ratings are shown. This suggests that there is a self-image problem on the part of the student that might appropriately be addressed on a priority basis. The example also shows sharply lower ratings by the employer than the teacher in three critical areas. This suggests a possible gap between what is taught in the classroom and what is needed on the job.

Figure 18 is a rating form used as suggested by Brolin (1976).

Job Tryout Evaluation Rating Form

Name of Trainee ____________________ Name of Company ____________________

Supervisor ____________________ Address ____________________

Job Title and Description of Work Performed: ____________________

____

____

Week of Evaluation: From __________ to __________ Weeks on Job: __________

Please rate the trainee on a four-point scale.

Trait	Good	Average	Fair	Poor
1. Attendance and Punctuality				
2. Speed of Work				
3. Accuracy of Work				
4. Neatness				
5. Ability to Work Without Much Supervision				
6. Safety Awareness and Practice				
7. Physical Capacities				
8. General Health				
9. Ability to Adjust to Varied Work Assignments				
10. Interest in Work				
11. Ability to Adapt to Work Environment				
12. Motivation (Initiative)				
13. Attention Span				
14. Reaction to Pressure				
15. Reaction to Constructive Criticism				
16. Ability to Follow Directions				
17. Ability to Retain Instructions				
18. Judgment and Problem-Solving Abilities				
19. Academic Skills				
20. Communication Skills (Speech)				
21. Cooperation with Supervisor				
22. Relationship With Coworkers				
23. Personal Grooming and Hygiene				
24. Appearance				
25. Potential for Work Performed				

Explanation of traits rated *fair* or *poor.*

Number

Recommendations

____

Work Supervisor

Figure 18. Job tryout evaluation rating form. Reprinted by permission from D. E. Broline. *Vocational Preparation of Retarded Citizens,* Charles E. Merrill, 1976.

Regardless of the format used, whether relatively simple, as is the Brolin version, or complex, as is the Kaplan version, the instrument must communicate clearly in terms of traits that *employers* consider important.

Student strengths and positive attributes should be stressed since employers care more about what a person *can* do than what he or she cannot do. That is not to say that a student's weakness should not be mentioned, but hopefully in such instances the phrasing of the evaluation can still be couched in constructive language. Thus, a student whose work quality is adversely effected by distractions (including "social" visiting by peers) might be described as follows: "Charlie's best work is accomplished when he is left alone or when co-workers' contacts pertain to the job itself."

Similarly, an employer cannot be blamed for being unenthusiastic about a student who, according to his teacher, "forgets oral instructions and has trouble reading printed instructions." Such an evaluative statement may indeed describe a mentally retarded individual if he or she has not been taught in a manner commensurate with his or her disability. A much better statement, and one that reflects the use of more appropriate instructional techniques, would be "has followed directions involving a series of ten steps after being given separate practice with each step and being provided with a simple checklist of the steps in the correct sequence."

In summary, school staff should carefully avoid the perpetuation of negative, stereotypic thinking about the handicapped. When a student graduates from a drafting course and *happens* to have a disabling condition, the latter fact in no way should diminish the importance of the former fact, *even if* not all the "normal" class activities were completed.

Certainly the way in which a student is presented to the business community will have much to do with whether he or she gets a chance to prove his or her worth. From the inception of a vocational curriculum and the assignment of a handicapped person into the program, the special educator and the vocational educator should be looking ahead and planning for the smoothest possible transition from training to employment for that individual.

APPROACHES TO JOB PLACEMENT

General Strategies

One general strategy that has been effectively used in progressive school districts is the designation of a professional person with vocational education and special education knowledge as a "Job Developer," a community liaison person whose primary function it is to place handicapped students in jobs for which they are qualified. When such persons are included in district staffing, the placements are probably best handled through that person rather than through the special educator/vocational educator instructional team. The implementation of California's Master Plan for special education should provide a considerable impetus for such staff assignments in that state.

There are a number of ways in which special educator/vocational educator instructional teams or a designated job developer might approach the placement of handicapped students in competitive employment as they leave the training setting. Briefly, these include the following:

1. *Selective placement,* emphasizing a network of cooperating employers and interested community supporters;
2. *Advertised placement,* emphasizing developed skills but not indicating the handicap;
3. *Preferential placement,* emphasizing that federal agencies and firms doing over $2,500 of business annually with the federal government are obligated to have an affirmative action program for hiring the handicapped;
4. *Coordinated placement,* emphasizing the involvement of the Department of Rehabilitation in locating jobs and placing the individual in accordance with his or her occupational training;
5. *Sheltered placement,* emphasizing jobs requiring limited skills, but with the hope of transitioning later to a regular business establishment even if at a reduced hourly wage rate;
6. *A combination of the above,* emphasizing whatever strategy seems most appropriate for the individual involved.

Selective Placement

This strategy presumes a thorough knowledge of the community in terms of work opportunities. It is based on the logical assumption that if an ideal match can be made between the student's capabilities and the job requirements (or, more specifically, the employer's idea of what he needs) then there is a greater likelihood that the student will succeed on the job.

A strength of this approach is that it operates in a manner that is very similar to work study, work experience, and cooperative education programs inasmuch as the employer's participation is cultivated in advance and there are no last-minute "surprises." It is quite possible within the selective placement approach that an employer who may be dubious and "on the fence" may become a staunch supporter if the initial placement involves a handicapped person whose work readiness is above average and who would be, in effect, a model employee.

Among the disadvantages of the selective placement approach are that it may limit the variety of job opportunities that are available to the handicapped student and it may not fully capitalize on the potential of the handicapped person in ways that were not apparent during the training program.

Advertised Placement

This strategy presumes that an employer is primarily interested in qualifications, including depth and breadth of experience in a related job. A variation of the advertised placement approach is used with a good deal of success in connection with handicapped persons who have received vocational training in San Jose, California. There, through the efforts of volunteer businessmen and educators, a newsletter is circulated through the business community informing them of qualified workers seeking employment. The following examples cover four diverse job categories, with the applicants having quite different qualifications.

Professional — G.B. 2015 Engineering Assistant-Computer Equipment. Design, development, testing, maintenance, and installation. Digital technology. Logic design. Degree in electronic technology.

Industrial — G.F. 5912 Electronic Assembler. One year experience in testing, wiring, inspection, packaging, and solder pot operation; uses all small hand tools easily.

Sales/Clerical — L.J. 9331 Billing Clerk. Ten key adding calculator, typing 35 on Selectric. Knows tariffs and bills of lading. Six years with moving and storage company.

Service — R.D. 1506 Food Serviceworker. One year experience in food service; can operate dishwasher, slicer, grill, mixer and cash register.

An advantage to this approach rests in that the individuals involved know they are being considered based on their qualifications because no hint of the nature of their disability appears in the newsletter. In effect, it is a way of saying "look, here's what I can do. Accept me on those terms and I'll do a good job for you."

A disadvantage that may exist in this approach is that it depends upon timing and even luck in finding an appropriate person/job match up. Clearly, if there is no response to the newsletter announcement then an alternative method for placement will have to be pursued.

Preferential Placement

This strategy presumes that federal, state and local government, and the majority of business firms who do business with the government, have a vested interest in seeking out and hiring the handicapped as required by law. Moreover, because these agencies have budgets and business organizations have profit and loss statements, neither type of organization would be likely to hire a handicapped person for "token" purposes but instead would seek ways to fully use his or her skills.

An advantage to preferential placement is that the trainee can be reasonably assured that such an agency or firm will be fair in reviewing his or her potential for career advancement. A possible disadvantage to this approach is that it tends to discount small business opportunities that may exist in the local community and that the individual might feel happier in joining.

Coordinated Placement

This strategy presumes that the Department of Rehabilitation has (as it should) a working relationship with the schools so that graduating handicapped students, if they so choose, can become eligible for services. In some states the Department maintains a close working relationship with the United States Employment Service or state level Employment Development Department. In effect, then, the coordinated approach can significantly broaden the school's knowledge of available job openings and provide additional support in seeking the most beneficial placement in relation to the student's potential.

An advantage to coordinated placement is that the rehabilitation counselor can often arrange for special assistance and special equipment if these must be acquired by the individual to get the job. For example, a blind applicant for an office job might need mobility training to get to this new destination independently, and the Department might be persuaded to purchase him or her an Optacon if the reading of ink print were an essential part of the job. A second advantage is that these organizations have an established network of employers with whom they have previously placed handicapped workers, thereby enhancing placement possibilities.

One disadvantage to this approach is that not all handicapped students are eligible to receive rehabilitation services. Current priorities lean toward those who are more severely handicapped and could not reasonably find a job on their own. Similarly, budget limitations within rehabilitation are such that useful equipment, e.g. a van equipped for wheelchair access, may not always be made available.

Sheltered Placement

This approach takes cognizance of the fact that some handicapped students will not be ready for employment once they leave school even though they may have received vocational training while they were enrolled. In such instances, community service organizations such as Goodwill or Easter Seal may be operating a sheltered workshop in which the individual could be productive while developing further vocational readiness.

An obvious advantage to the sheltered workshop approach is that it gives the individual a desirable alternative to idleness, and it can provide needed opportunities for social interaction, further skill development, or work habit improvement.

A disadvantage is that it is not a suitable placement strategy for all individuals who happen to be handicapped, especially those whose handicaps are not severe. Because the workshop pay rates are generally low (being based on piece rates in most cases), it is important that persons having the potential to "make it" independently in the competitive job market should be given that preferred option.

Other Placement Methods

Opportunities often develop that cannot be predicted in advance. They can be encouraged, however, by increasing the possibilities for favorable results. The case of Ignacio Navarro of Oceanside, California is a good illustration.

Lacking a high school diploma, a naturalized citizen of Mexican extraction, and experienced as a cook, Ignacio could not get permanent work in his field in this country. Having lost his left hand and part of his arm in a factory accident, Ignacio eventually was referred to the Oceanside Regional Occupational Program by the Department of Rehabilitation. There he took a nine-week electronics assembly course. Just before he had completed the course he was contacted for a job interview by one of the ROP advisors who happened to be the personnel manager for a local electronics firm. Ignacio now inspects and tests electrical components using a special testing machine and holding delicate electronic tools in the clamps of his prosthetic device.

In summary, no one method of job placement will work in all cases, and each method has some advantages as well as disadvantages. The special educator/vocational educator instructional team are in the most informed position, however, to recommend a course of action for a given individual. Their knowledge of the student is an important asset, and their importance as resource persons should not be overlooked even after the handicapped individual has gotten a job.

In the same vein, by keeping in touch with their successfully employed graduates, the special educator/vocational educator team can occasionally invite them to be guests in the classroom, giving younger handicapped students encouragement and an incentive to develop their own competencies.

ADDRESSING SPECIFIC PLACEMENT PROBLEMS

Job Applications, Interviews, and Testing

Unless one is personally handicapped, it is difficult to imagine how frustrating and serious this "routine" process can become. How does the mentally retarded, or the spastic, or the blind individual fill out the job application form? How does the deaf person phone to arrange an interview? How does the speech-impaired or the deaf person carry out the interview? What tests given by the organization to establish job qualifications are fair and which are not? These are not easy questions and there are no easy answers.

As a basic principle, the special educator/vocational educator team should address these problems *early,* taking into account the nature of the person's disability and the likely areas of difficulty that would be encountered at the time that jobs are being applied for. With this advance knowledge, training can be given within the school context to help prepare the handicapped person for these real-life situations.

Application Forms

A stumbling block for many young people (including nonhandicapped as well as handicapped) is the vocabulary that they will encounter on standard application forms. As a first step in preparing the students, the special educator may find it helpful to give them practice with the most commonly encountered words.

employer	defect	unemployed	compensation	postal	phy.
employed	nature	certificate	classification	permanent	profession
employment	record	social security	canning	quit	presently
present	attended	descent	card	qualifications	principal
phone	female	details	draft	receive	coast
application	male	item	data	recent	concern
mo.	birthplace	length	disabilities	reserve	choice
rate	degree	arrested	earnings	released	citizenship
relatives	discharge	complete	employ	retail	character
applied	seasonal	disposition	factory	regular	corresponden
previous	wage	graduate	firm	recommended	companies
completed	former	grammar	formal	referred	doctors
social sec. no.	emergency	health	furnish	shift	serial
yr.	foreign	hernia	guard	union	skin
business	odd	handed	G.I.	unimportant	stationary
single	previously	whether	graduation	unemployment	spouse
no.	references	local	Gov't.	univer. (university)	salary
zone	veteran	misc.	grad	void	suggestion
college	supervisor	marital	hobbies	vehicle	specialization
height	entry	offense	history	vocational	summarize
list	information	order	hobby	short	example
weight	apprenticeship	resort	illness	sales	exam
applicant	active	traffic	issue	specialized	etc.
dependents	described	university	identification	statements	employee
physical	duty	violations	interviews	applying	advertisement
type	discharged	available	insurance	attach	agency
widowed	graduated	alien	injury	area	accord
divorced	handicaps	academic	inclusive	acquired	form
position	including	forces	knowledge	apply	ink
relationship	location	regardless	legal	attending	mailing
separated	monthly	ckd.		authorization	unknown
middle	maiden	disability	marines	wounded	usually
signature	notify	additional	marriage	reversed	written
course	naturalized	subjects	major	reached	retirement
dept.	personal	emp.	motor	registration	P.O.
education	remarks	initial	nationality	recently	county
experience	status	Negro	naturalization	recreation	tel. no.
military	trade	sex	notified	refer	typewriters
occupation	sal. (salary)	specify	operation	percentage	except
service	s. s. no.	accidents	petition	point	administratio
training	rank	briefly	prefer	photo	
citizen	persons	bus. (business)	photograph	prompted	

Figure 19. Words to be taught, in the order of their frequency on applications (words on Gates-Thorndike third grade list not included). Reprinted by permission from R. J. Wilson, Job Application Vocabulary, *The Pointer*, Winter, 1974.

Wilson (1974) has researched more than 100 application blanks and has compiled a priority list of words. Figure 19 shows Wilson's listing in the order of their frequency on application forms. Wilson points out that some words can be taught through similar meanings, others through structural analysis, and still others through content, experience, and practice. Hopefully, many of the words can be made meaningful through being incorporated in the context of conversation and practice with actual forms rather than through rote drill of isolated terms.

Physical problems of filling out forms and sensory problems that prevent their being read are probably best overcome by using a helping individual. Only rarely would a circumstance arise when this would not be feasible. In any case, denying employment through prejudicial hiring practices is not legal. Therefore, only where the job itself is much like the filling out of the application would there be any justification for requesting this form completion by the applicant. Again, adaptive tools and aids are often available to help the individual perform the work once he or she has been hired, but not before.

To illustrate, the fact that a blind person could not see the application or fill it out by hand should not be a reason to deny a job to that person. For example, blind clerks can use an Opticon attached to a typewriter to read and fill out many types of business forms. The Sensory Aids Foundation of Palo Alto, California, for example, has placed over 100 blind persons in jobs over a three-year period, with only six no longer employed. Using appropriate assistive devices, these blind persons have gotten jobs that are heavily dependent on the printed word, including the following:

Human Services Aide	Loan Officer Trainee (Bank)
Reporter (Newspaper)	Office Products Sales Trainee
Chief Economist	Coordinator for Blind and Partially Sighted Students (College)
Radio Operator	
Computer Programmer	Word Processing Operator
Receptionist	Vocational Rehabilitation Counselor

Supervisor (Medical Center)

TV Repairman

Music Teacher

Physical Therapist

Library Assistant

Insurance Salesman

Machinist

Electronics Technician

Radio Broadcaster

Teacher

Radio Archivist

Office Manager

College Clerk

Clerk Typist

Medical Transcriber

Bank Supervisor

Engineer

Machine Operator

Police Dispatcher

Systems Analyst

Music Therapist

Executive Secretary

Bank Credit Verifier

Information Service Representative

Claims Examiner (Insurance Company)

Deputy Clerk (Municipal Court)

Mental Health Education Consultant

TSPS Operator (Telephone Company)

Engineer, Chemistry and Encapsulation

Quality Assurance/Assembler (for Electronics Company)

Radio Production Engineer

Disability Specialist and Program Coordinator

Reservationist (Major Airline Carrier)

Electronic Engineering Assistant

Biomedical Equipment Technician

Associate Program Writer

Operations Supervisor (Social Security Admin.)

Switchboard Operator

Special Services Assistant

Regional Staff Assistant

Small Appliance Repairman

Darkroom Technician

Physical Science Technician

Telephone Service Representative

Job Information Specialist

Interviews

Whenever possible, preliminary visits to the employer can help to allay problems that would otherwise occur for more seriously handicapped individuals. Lesser handicapped individuals, on the other hand, might be able to "go it alone," thus demonstrating from the outset that they will be self-reliant on the job.

In making preliminary calls, the emphasis should be placed on helping the employer to ask reasonable questions in reasonable ways. He or she may be quite unfamiliar with the handicapping condition and could easily (1) feel a sense of awkwardness and embarassment that interferes with candor in the interview, (2) misunderstand the dividing line between discriminatory and relevant questioning, (3) wrongly assume things about the person's capabilities, and (4) be unaware of compensatory aids and assistive techniques that are available which could relieve certain "how to" problems later on the job.

One helpful source of information on appropriate interviewing procedures is the United States Employment Service, in the Department of Labor. A series of brief booklets appropriate for use with the following handicaps has been developed:

- mental retardation
- heart disease
- diabetes
- mentally restored
- legal blindness and blindness
- hearing impairments
- epilepsy
- alcoholism
- visual impairments

Each guide contains a description (in nonmedical terms) of the handicapping condition and information that is helpful in making judgments about the employability of such persons on an individual basis. Note that the booklets in no way are substitutes for medical or performance appraisals used in establishing job qualifications.

Insofar as possible, the United States Employment Service tries to be sure that at least one person in each local office has been identified to serve the handicapped. School personnel may want to become acquainted with this person and may also find it helpful to examine the highly informative United States Employment Service document entitled *Placing Handicapped Applicants: An Employment Service Handbook,* which many community level placement specialists will already have in their offices.

Testing

Being handicapped does not excuse a person from being tested in job-relevant ways. For this testing to be fair, however, the applicant should be able to use in the test situation any adaptive aid or procedure that might enable him or her to do the job itself. Common sense should prevail when decisions are being made about testing and its relationship to occupational placement.

One way around the dilemma of being able to prove job worthiness in lieu of pre-testing (when the nature of the job permits this alternative) is to have the handicapped employee try the job on a conditional basis for a brief period of time. Such an approach avoids placing either the employer or the handicapped employee in an untenable position if the person/job match-up is unworkable. Job re-engineering, making modifications to the work station, or constructing specially designed aids and appliances all represent constructive alternatives even when the initial person/job match-up seems less than perfect.

As an example, Asher and Asher (1976) have described the following work site accommodation for a quadriplegic worker:

> Maryland quadriplegic Don Taylor's hand movement is so limited that without special aids he cannot perform such otherwise elementary tasks as writing with a pen, operating a cassette dictation machine, or using a conventional telephone. Taylor manages writing implements with a fitted holder fashioned out of stainless steel; he uses both hands to write. His employer has provided him with a speaker phone, which he dials with a pencil gripped by the holder.

In another example, Los Angeles attorney Jack Achtenberg, a quadriplegic with no use of his arms or legs, uses a specially modified Sony dictation machine. The machine has a voice-actuated microphone and magnetic switches, which Jack operates by holding a magnet-tipped stick in his teeth. (Interestingly, Sony Corporation has demonstrated the feasibility of adapting equipment for workers by staffing one of its plants in Tokyo with the handicapped.)

The adaptive approaches in these two examples illustrate how a person can carry out activities that might, at first, appear impossible. Obviously, not all activities lend themselves to adaptive techniques, yet a surprising number of solutions can be found if the special educator/vocational educator team will use their own imagination and, when appropriate, refer specific problems to regional rehabilitation engineering services or other potentially helpful local organizations.

FOLLOW-UP AND SUPPORT ON THE JOB

As has been mentioned, handicapped students who enter the world of work may find it helpful to look upon the special educator and the vocational educator as resource persons to whom they can turn for advice on problems encountered on the job. Since there are practical limits on the amount of time and effort that instructors can reasonably spend with graduates from their programs, it is important that students be taught how to cope with any on-the-job problems that can be anticipated.

Some of the on-the-job areas of concern include

- getting along with co-workers and supervisors, including ways of heading off interpersonal problems;
- knowing how to ask for help when it is needed, including having a special tool made to enable recurring tasks to be performed;
- taking precautions when and if hazardous situations arise;
- maintaining reliability and dependability, including punctuality and attentiveness to deadlines;
- maintaining high productivity and meeting job standards.

Each of these areas (and other areas not listed) can be addressed in part during training prior to getting the job. Since unique situations characterize every job, no surefire formulas can be offered. Nevertheless, some ideas have proven workable in a number of situations. Some typical problems and some of the possible alternative responses will be discussed here.

PROBLEM 1. A line supervisor and co-workers on an assembly line object to the transfer of an epileptic to their work team. They say that she would be absent a lot, would be a hazard to herself and others, and they would not know what to do in case she "has a fit."

Possible responses might include the following:

a. Refer to a Department of Labor Study (#923) that showed no significant differences existed between epileptic and unimpaired workers in respect to attendance and accident records. Also point out that Workmen's Compensation Laws are based on the industry and total accident rates of employees and are not changed when a handicapped person is employed. Further, a 1968 study by Goldwater showed that 72 percent of workers so handicapped (epilepsy and cerebral vascular disease) had job performance ratings equal to or better than co-workers.
b. Refer to the individual's work record prior to the transfer.
c. Suggest an orientation meeting at which the supervisor and employer can be familiarized with the symptoms. Such a meeting could involve another epileptic who has successfully overcome the problem. If appropriate, point out the extent to which the condition can be (or is) controlled through medication.

PROBLEM 2. A quadriplegic worker in an employment department is responsible for interviewing applicants. His work requires filling out forms, use of the telephone, maintaining records, and moving through the office, none of which he can do efficiently, even though he has a powered wheelchair (it does not fit the aisles). He has special arm supports, one of which is rigged with a wrist-activated, three-jawed chuck, which enables him to hold a pen in his fingertips. His chief problems are his limited access to materials (necessitating his supervisor to help him several times a day) and the difficulty of moving about the office.

The approach to improving his efficiency of performance (a

50% increase was achieved) involved the following steps:

a. His regular desk was replaced with a lazy Susan type of desk that was electically powered, operated by micro-switches, and had ample room for his wheelchair to move into position. His work space was increased 1000 percent, and he no longer needed extra help from the supervisor to reach documents.
b. His wheelchair was replaced with a speedier model, which had a new type of arm support requiring less overall width to traverse an aisle.

PROBLEM 3. A construction and landscape maintenance company has agreed to hire three mentally retarded workers on an exploratory basis. Some of the union workers are not very receptive, claiming that work standards would drop and that they would have to do the work of the mentally retarded.

Possible strategies might include the following:

a. Cite George Meany's statement as head of the AFL/CIO that "the AFL-CIO is committed to the principle that everyone should have full opportunity to achieve his maximum personal development and fulfillment. Unions participate in the establishment of training programs and other community service facilities to enable the worker who is mentally retarded to take his place as a wage earner and a positive factor in our economy and society."
b. Pass out brochures (to the employer and to the employees) citing tips for working effectively with the mentally retarded; contact the local chapter of the National Association for Retarded Citizens for assistance of this sort.
c. Organize the mentally retarded workers into a team of their own, under the supervision of an able and interested worker, and give each person a steady, noncompetitive assignment on the team. (In San Mateo, California, for example, such a crew cares for the grounds of an apartment complex and a large community hospital. The quality of work at these sites can be used as tangible evidence of their ability to perform the work, noting that it was done with a spirit of cooperation and mutual support.)

Facilitating the Transition from School to Work

Vocational training involves much more than skills development if the transition from school to work is to be accomplished smoothly and with a maximum number of successful job placements. Toward that end, the special educator and vocational educator have complementary roles to play.

GOAL	SPECIAL EDUCATOR FUNCTION	VOCATIONAL EDUCATOR FUNCTION
Provide appropriate follow-up and support on the job and at home	Assure transportation to vocational experience and/or work station in community	Develop and maintain list of cooperating and potential employers
	Assure that independent living skills have been developed and are maintained	Arrange for linkages to vocational experience and/or work station in community
	Coordination with Department of Rehabilitation to provide follow-up services	Prepare list of job-relevant student competencies and strengths
		Evaluate individual's performance on the job (including any implications for possible future curriculum revisions)
		Suggest adaptive techniques and guidelines to employer

It can be seen in these examples that the team relationship between the special educator and the vocational educator is an important one. At each successive stage, from initial student intake to the time that the student enters the working world, complementary skills are needed by the instructional team. Figure 20 serves as a reminder of the major points to be emphasized in this cooperative approach to instruction. These points are (1) meeting individual needs in the area of work habits such as dependability and using time productively, (2) meeting individual needs in the area of skill development, including any adaptive techniques that may be required, (3) en-

Figure 20. Principal elements of vocational training. A. Developing good work habits and reliability. B. Learning technical skills and safety procedures.

→

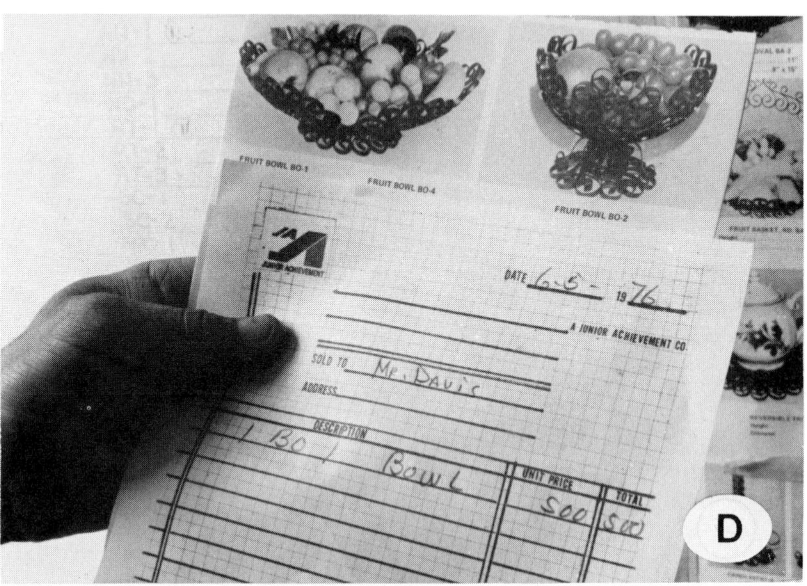

C. Building self-reliance to meet requirements. D. Gaining work experience and interpersonal skills.

couraging the individual to develop greater self-reliance on a task, though still working in cooperation with others, and (4) helping the student to gain meaningful work exposure and job opportunities that reflect his or her career interests and goals.

The deaf student shown in Figure 20 is enrolled in a regular vocational program at the high school level in San Jose, California. His vocational instructor does not sign, but there is no lack of communication in the classroom. There will be no lack of preparedness on the part of this student as he enters the working world upon graduation.

PART IV

SUPPLEMENTAL FORMS

VOCATIONAL EVALUATION

Vocational evaluation involves several interrelated and important factors. Personal and social characteristics, interests, and aptitudes are important indicators of possible occupational fields that merit consideration. Similarly, predictors of how well the person will perform on the job include work attitudes, work habits, situational assessments, and performance assessments using simulations of the job or actual job samples.

The following adapted form is a comprehensive, but simplified, means of evaluating these various vocational indicators. It should be noted that this form in no way substitutes for the more detailed information that may result from the use of vocational tests or behavioral observations with work sample systems.

Job-relevant personal qualities	*Outstanding*	*Satisfactory*	*Needs Improvement*
1. Honest	____	____	____
2. Courteous	____	____	____
3. Neat	____	____	____
4. Persevering	____	____	____
5. Adaptable	____	____	____
6. Energetic	____	____	____
7. Quick	____	____	____
8. Careful	____	____	____
9. Attentive	____	____	____
10. Dependable	____	____	____
Job-relevant behaviors			
1. Follows safety precautions	____	____	____
2. Completes tasks	____	____	____
3. Uses time productively	____	____	____
4. Accepts criticism	____	____	____
5. Exhibits initiative	____	____	____
6. Functions independently	____	____	____
7. Cooperative with others	____	____	____
8. Follows directions	____	____	____
9. Adheres to work schedule	____	____	____
10. Performs well under stress	____	____	____

Job-relevant aptitudes and abilities	*Excellent*	*Fair*	*Poor*
1. Computational aptitude	____	____	____
2. Mechanical aptitude	____	____	____
3. Comprehension	____	____	____
4. Communication	____	____	____
5. Form perception	____	____	____
6. Color discrimination	____	____	____
7. Space perception	____	____	____
8. Manual dexterity	____	____	____
9. Finger dexterity	____	____	____
10. Hand-eye coordination	____	____	____
11. Eye-hand-foot coordination	____	____	____
12. Physical strength and agility	____	____	____

Job-relevant interests and preferences	*Liked*	*Neutral*	*Disliked*
1. Working with people	____	____	____
2. Working with plants or animals	____	____	____
3. Working with objects and things	____	____	____
4. Working with abstract ideas	____	____	____
5. Working with language	____	____	____
6. Working with machines and tools	____	____	____
7. Work that requires decision making	____	____	____
8. Work offering high prestige	____	____	____
9. Work having tangible outcomes	____	____	____
10. Work that is highly structured	____	____	____
11. Work that is physically demanding	____	____	____
12. Work that involves travel	____	____	____

THE VOCATIONAL EDUCATOR'S PLAN FOR ACTION

The vocational educator can use the following pages as a reminder and a plan for action for *each handicapped student* in the class. Each section represents a major step in a careful process of *Planning Instruction, Implementing Instruction,* and *Describing Instructional Outcomes.* An additional section is designed to facilitate *Employment and Follow-up* when the student has completed the course.

PLANNING INSTRUCTION

Knowing About the Handicapped Student

A. The student's name (or code number) is ______________________________

The student's disability is called, ______________________________

A basic definition is ______________________________

____

Are there associated problems or disabilities? What are they?

____

B. What physical, emotional, or mental characteristics are *clearly* evident that would limit employability? Could any of these *limiting* characteristics be modified through training, use of a device, or environmental modifications? (Specify)

____

____

C. What evidence can you find that suggests whether the student *copes* with the handicap effectively and is able to "get things done?"

____

____

D. What are the student's *existing* interests, demonstrated abilities, and strengths as revealed by existing school records or through interviews?

____

____

____

E. What have you learned from the *special educator* relating to medication, attendance, and procedures to follow if health care is required in the classroom or work station?

____

____

Additional notes: ______________________________

____

____

Knowing Yourself

A. Do you usually modify your regular class procedures to accommodate *individual differences*? If not, why not? If so, what modifications do you make?

____

____

B. Are you worried about the prospect of having a handicapped student in your classroom? If so, what concerns you the most? Discuss your main concerns.

____

____

____

C. What underlying reason(s) are there for these feelings and concerns? What might be done to modify the situation?

____

____

____

D. When dealing with the handicapped student, how will you *check yourself* to be sure that your feelings don't cause any inappropriate reaction (pity, condescension, rejection, etc.), but rather that your actions create a favorable learning environment?

____

____

____

E. What are the greatest *strengths* you have as an instructor that will be important to the handicapped student?

____

____

Additional notes: ______________________________

____

____

____

Job/Task Analysis

A. Based on your knowledge of the *current job market,* what types of jobs in your occupational area might be open to the handicapped student for which he or she could be qualified?

____

____

____

B. Have you prepared a *breakdown of the tasks* involved in these jobs? Which tasks could the handicapped person do and which would be particularly difficult?

____

____

____

C. Can you give the student any examples of other *handicapped* persons who have been employed in this type of occupation? (Specify)

____

____

____

D. To what extent is there a possibility of *re-engineering of the job* so that the very difficult (inefficiently performed) tasks could be eliminated or reassigned to another person?

____

____

E. After comparing the job tasks to your course of study and class activities, what task level problems are apt to occur in *both* situations? What might you do about them?

____

____

____

Additional notes: ______________________________

____

____

Cooperative Goal Setting

A. Based on your review of the goals and objectives in the student's *Individualized Educational Program* (IEP) and related discussions with the special educator, what priorities should be set?

____

____

____

B. Based on your *analysis* of the job market and the handicapped student's potential, what types of vocational assessment and counseling would be appropriate? (Specify)

____

____

____

C. What aspects of the student's vocational assessment have a direct bearing on the setting of *realistic course objectives and timetables*?

____

____

____

D. What *short term goals* have been cooperatively set?

____

____

E. When will you assess whether the short term goals have been accomplished? What *performance criteria* will you use? How do these criteria differ from the criteria applied to other students?

____

____

____

Additional notes: _______________

____

____

____

Needed Course Modifications

A. Considering your curriculum, what course content modifications are needed relative to the student's *skills development*? Decide what information and steps are important and avoid unnecessary, time-consuming diversions.

____

____

____

B. What course modifications are needed relative to the student's *general understanding of the world of work*?

____

____

____

C. What course content modifications are needed relative to the student's *work habits, interpersonal relationships and personal safety*?

____

____

____

D. What *work experiences* would be appropriate for this student? (Identify these as specifically as possible.)

____

____

____

Additional notes: ______________________________

____

____

____

Barrier Removal

A. What *equipment* modifications or additions are important to help the student in assigned tasks?

____

____

____

B. What *facility* modifications or additions are appropriate to accommodate the student? Consider access to the class, the classroom itself, the work station, and related facilities such as storage areas.

____

____

____

C. What *transportation* assistance is advisable to enable the student to reach the class or the work experience location?

____

____

____

D. What *communication* barriers can be anticipated in the classroom or at the work station, and what might be done to alleviate these problems?

____

____

____

Additional notes: ______________________________

____

____

____

Helpful Resources

A. What special *instructional materials* might be obtained to help the student master your course? Where can you get them?

B. What *persons* should you involve as advisors, interpreters or aides, or teammates for this student? (Consider professional persons, classroom paraprofessionals, parents, and capable vocational students.)

C. What *outside agencies* may provide special help or funds? What specific help could be given this student?

Additional notes:

IMPLEMENTING INSTRUCTION

Student Assessment Following Initial Instructional Period

A. To what extent did the student reach the goals that were cooperatively set for this *initial* period?

1. Tasks accomplished on time? ______________________________

2. Performance skills satisfactory? ______________________________

3. Work habits satisfactory? ______________________________

4. Social relationships satisfactory? ______________________________

5. Other goals met? ______________________________

____

B. For those areas where the student's progress was *unsatisfactory*, what adjustments should be made in the goals for the next period?

____

____

____

C. For those areas where the student's progress was *satisfactory*, was the student sufficiently challenged to reach his or her *full* potential?

____

____

D. What is the student's *self-appraisal* so far?

____

____

____

Additional notes: ______________________________

____

____

____

Initial Assessment of Yourself and Significant Others

A. In the initial period of instruction were you able to project a *positive, supportive attitude*? If not, what prevented it? How can this factor be changed for the next instructional period?

____

____

____

B. Did you find yourself constantly concerned about the handicapped student or were you able to take the student's *individual differences* in stride? (Explain)

____

____

C. Did you get the kind of *back-up help* you wanted from other persons?

1. Special educator ______________________________
2. Classroom interpreter or aide ______________________________
3. Other students ______________________________
4. Administrators ______________________________
5. Other support persons ______________________________

D. If this student is in a *work experience* setting, how did the employer and co-workers react to the student?

____

____

____

Additional notes: ______________________________

____

____

____

Revisions of Instructional Strategy

A. Based on the initial instructional period, what *goals* seem appropriate for the student in the remainder of the course?

____

____

____

B. Based on the results of the initial instructional *period,* what changes are appropriate for the remainder of the course to best meet the needs of the handicapped student?

1. In the curriculum? ______________________________

____

____

2. In the equipment, facility, or transportation? ______________

____

____

3. In the materials, resources, or agencies? ________________

____

____

4. In your instructional approach? ____________________

____

____

____

Additional notes: ______________________________

____

____

____

DESCRIBING INSTRUCTIONAL OUTCOMES

Student's Development of Employable Skills

A. During this course, the handicapped student has developed the following *employable skills, subskills,* and *levels of performance*:

(Example) Skill: *decorates baked goods*

Subskills: *applies icing, rosettes, lettering*

Quality of performance: *creative, thorough*

1. Skill: ______________________

   Subskills: ______________________

   Quality of performance: ______________________

2. Skill: ______________________

   Subskills: ______________________

   Quality of performance: ______________________

3. Skill: ______________________

   Subskills: ______________________

   Quality of performance: ______________________

4. Skill: ______________________

   Subskills: ______________________

   Quality of performance: ______________________

5. Skill: ______________________

   Subskills: ______________________

   Quality of performance: ______________________

6. Skill: ______________________

   Subskills: ______________________

   Quality of performance: ______________________

B. List any skills that need *further development* to increase the student's employability. To whom would you refer the student for special help?

____

____

Additional notes: ______________________

Student's Development of Work Attitudes and Habits

A. During this course, the handicapped student has developed the following *work habits*:

(Examples) *Consistently punctual, follows safety precautions*

1. ____________________
2. ____________________
3. ____________________
4. ____________________
5. ____________________
6. ____________________
7. ____________________
8. ____________________

B. During this course, the handicapped student has developed the following work-relevant attitudes:

(Examples) *Relates well to others, cooperates willingly*

1. ____________________
2. ____________________
3. ____________________
4. ____________________
5. ____________________
6. ____________________
7. ____________________
8. ____________________

C. List any work habits that need *further development* to increase the student's employability? Who can provide the needed assistance?

____

____

Additional notes: ____________________

____

____

Overall Assessment of Outcomes

A. In *your opinion*, what student benefits or gains have been made as a result of this course?

____

____

____

B. In the *student's opinion*, what benefits or gains have been made as a result of this course?

____

____

____

C. How have *you* personally gained by this experience?

____

____

____

D. What is your point of view about *future* experiences in instructing handicapped students in regular vocational education classes?

____

____

____

Additional notes: ________________________________

____

____

____

EMPLOYMENT AND FOLLOW-UP

Work Placement Considerations

A. Is there a favorable *precedent* for placement in this job situation, such as previous handicapped employee or trainee, or favorable employer viewpoint?

____

____

____

B. To what extent has the student been *sufficiently trained* for the type of work and level of responsibility required at the work situation?

____

____

____

C. Are there problems to be worked out *in advance,* such as transportation, co-worker attitudes, etc.?

____

____

____

D. What is an appropriate *trial period* to give the trainee a fair chance without "locking in" the employer?

____

____

E. What *criteria* can you and the employer agree on, in advance, for judging the trainee's performance on the job?

____

____

____

Additional notes: ______________________________

____

____

____

Performance on the Job

A. The job tasks performed at an *outstanding* level include:

____

____

____

____

B. The job tasks performed at an *adequate* level include:

____

____

____

____

C. The job tasks performed at an *inadequate* level include:

____

____

____

____

D. Other appraisals of trainee performance that affect *employment potential* include:

____

____

Additional notes: ______________________________

____

____

____

REFERENCES

Accent Special Publications: *Accent on Living-Buyer's Guide.* Bloomington, IL: Cheever Publications, 1978.

American Automobile Association: *The Handicapped Driver's Mobility Guide.* Falls Church, VA, 1978.

American Foundation for the Blind: *Aids and Appliances for the Blind and Visually Handicapped,* 24th ed. New York, 1978-79.

Asher, Janet and Asher, Jules: How to accommodate workers in wheelchairs. *Job Safety and Health,* October, 1976 (President's Committee on Employment of the Handicapped).

Barbacovi, Don R. and Clelland, Richard W.: *Public Law 94-142-Special Education in Transition.* Arlington, VA, American Association of School Administrators, (1977).

Bolton, Brian B. (Ed.): *Handbook of Measurement and Evaluation in Rehabilitation.* Baltimore, Univ Park, 1976.

Brolin, Donn E.: *Vocational Preparation of Retarded Citizens.* Columbus, Merrill, 1976.

Bureau of Education for the Handicapped: *Proceedings of the Conference on Research Needs Related to the Career Education of the Handicapped.* Washington, U.S. Office of Education. 1975.

Bureau of the Budget: *Standard Industrial Classification Manual.* Washington, Executive Office of the President, 1976.

Buros, Oliver Krisen: *Vocational Tests and Reviews.* Highland Park, NJ, Gryphon Pr, 1975.

California State Department of Education: *California State Plan for Vocational Education.* Sacramento, 1976.

Dahl, Peter R., Appleby, Judith A., and Lipe, Dewey: *Mainstreaming Guidebook for Vocational Educators.* Salt Lake City, Olympus Pub Co, 1978 (Copyright by American Institutes for Research in the Behavioral Sciences, Palo Alto, CA).

Employment and Training Administration: *Dictionary of Occupational Titles,* 4th ed. Washington, U.S. Dept. of Labor, 1977. (3rd ed., 1965)

Flanagan, John C.: *Career Handbook.* Monterey, CTB McGraw Hill, 1976.

Hantman, Paula: Physically handicapped are great word processors. *The Office,* 44, 58, November, 1977.

Holland, John: Vocational guidance for everyone. *Educational Researcher, 3*:9-15, 1974.

Hoyt, Kenneth B., Evans, Rupert N., Mackin, Edward F., and Mangum, Garth L: *Career Education—What It Is and How To Do It.* Salt Lake

City, Olympus Pub Co, 1972.

Human Resources Center: *Hand Controls and Assistive Devices for the Physically Disabled Driver.* Albertson, NY, Human Resources Center, 1977.

Johnson, E.W.: Let's look at the child—not the audiogram. In Northcott, Winifred H.: *The Hearing Impaired Child in a Regular Classroom.* Washington, Alexander Graham Bell Assoc. for the Deaf, 1973.

Johnson, S.R. and Johnson, R.B.: *Developing Individualized Instructional Material.* Palo Alto, Westinghouse Learn, 1970.

Kaplan, Stanley: Toward teaching and counseling excellence — A student profile. *Teaching Exceptional Children, 10:*18-23, 1977.

Kenney, Eleanore T.: Learning disability — What it is and is not. *Educational Leadership, 32:*507-511, 1975.

Kokaska, Charles: Career awareness for handicapped students in elementary schools. *Career Development for Exceptional Individuals, 1:*25-35, 1978.

Love, Don et al.: *Vocational Education and the Physically Handicapped.* Los Angeles, Los Angeles City College, 1971.

Massachusetts Department of Education: *Regulations 766* (Regulations for the Implementation of Chapter 766 of the Acts of 1972 — the Comprehensive Special Education Law). Boston, 1978.

Moyer, John R. and Dardig, Jill C.: Practical task analysis for special educators. *Teaching Exceptional Children, 11:*16-18, 1978.

Olympus Research Corp.: *An Assessment of Vocational Education Programs for the Handicapped under Part B of the 1968 Amendments to the Vocational Education Act.* Salt Lake City, Olympus Pub Co, 1974.

O'Neil, Sharon L.: *Occupational Survival Skills: Implications for Job Maintenance and Mobility.* Urbana, U of Ill Pr, 1976.

Parker, Randall M. and Hansen, Carl E.: Aptitude and achievement tests. In Bolton, Brian B. (Ed.): *Handbook of Measurement and Evaluation in Rehabilitation.* Baltimore, Univ Park, 1976.

Perlman, Leonard: *The Person With Epilepsy—Life Style, Needs, Expectations.* Chicago, National Epilepsy League, 1977.

Phelps, I. Allen: *Instructional Development for Special Needs Learners — An Inservice Resource Guide.* Urbana, U of Ill Pr, 1976.

Russell, Gene: *A Five County Vocational Skills Training Program for the Blind.* Santa Cruz, CA, County Office of Education, 1972.

Shigley, Ron J.: *An Overview of Vocational Education—Vocational Evaluation Unit.* North Carolina Department of Public Instruction and the Thoms Rehabilitation Hospital, Asheville. Asheville Orthopedic Hospital, 1976.

Sinick, Daniel: Training, job placement, and follow-up. In Malikan, David and Rusalem, Herbert: *Vocational Rehabilitation of the Disabled — An Overview.* New York, NYU Pr, 1969.

Szoke, Claire O. and Vest, Sharon: *To Serve Those Who Are Handicapped—Procedures and Format to Implement a Model Career Education*

Program for the Handicapped, rev. ed. Champaign and Springfield, IL, Technical Education Research Center, Midwest and Springfield Public Schools, 1975.

U.S. Employment Service: *Placing Handicapped Applicants — An Employment Service Handbook.* Washington, U.S. Dept. of Labor, Feb, 1978.

Washington Report. American Foundation for the Blind, NY, 1978 (newsletter).

Weisgerber, Robert (Ed.): *Vocational Education-Teaching the Handicapped In Regular Classes.* Reston, VA, Council for Exceptional Children, 1978.

Wentling, Tim L., Peak, Laurie, M., Jensen, Terry A., and Russo, Rocco P.: *Resource Directory for Teacher Education in Vocational Special Needs.* Minneapolis, Minnesota Research and Development Center for Vocational Education, U. of Minnesota, 1978.

Wilson, Richard J.: Job application vocabulary. *The Pointer, 19:*114-115, 1974.

INDEX

W